How to LIVE a Vibrant Life

By

MICHAEL KEITH HENSON, LMFT

LCCN: 2025910284

Case ID: 1-14924663301

E-Book: 978-1-300-25129-3

Paperback: 978-1-300-25128-6

Hardcover: 978-1-300-25127-9

PREFACE

I am grateful for the privilege to have worked as Director of Rapha Treatment 28-day Inpatient Psychiatric and Substance Abuse Rehab Center. A lot of what I learned to write this book came from my work with Rapha, two previous marriages, and many of my friends like Jim N., Deb W., several pastors, two mentors – Jerry M. and Dr. Lester, and private practice clients. I want to say "THANK YOU" to you all for your wisdom and insight.

INTRODUCTION

Introduction to the book: I am a licensed mental health therapist, life counselor, and couple's coach. Much of what I am going to describe to the reader to help you, I personally have lived out my huge struggle with life. I am excited about the privilege to share this valuable information with readers to help you overcome your insecurity of self-esteem, to explain how to understand yourself better, to recognize responding versus reacting to life concepts, to guide you with three concentric circles so that you may choose more healthy, productive and successful decisions. Later in the book, I will give you the necessary skills and tools to help you recover and reconcile your relationship with others. You will discover clarity in purpose, how you communicate, and why you do what you do. I'm convinced you can and will be transformed by recognizing and applying these truths from my presentation. I count it a privilege to share what has taken me a life time to learn and articulate.

Is it your goal to pursue happiness and peace of mind? Is your strategy or your system working for you?

How do you make decisions? What is the process and the elements to consider to determine if and when you have made a wise, effective decision?

The **goal of this book** is to assist the reader in understanding how individuals process information while influenced by their own personal perspectives to arrive at decisions that affect positive, neutral, or negative outcomes. Observe the three concentric circles diagram. This author wants the reader to discover the reactions and responses, which are the two types of behaviors manifested. Take the journey to see the behaviors of reacting or responding that evolve from the free will in the soul. The will, consisting of the endocrine, nerve, and immune systems, gather manifestations of the emotions derived from the Amygdala and the thoughts created by the mind, not the Brain. The mind and the emotions in the soul are impacted by the beliefs in the depth of a person's spirit. So now, this author wants to break these general concepts into more specific details to enlighten the reader about the benefits of making a radical transformation to a healthier, more vibrant life.

The goal of this author is to inform the reader that a person is possessed by three Characteristics: body, soul, and spirit. When a person is confronted with the triggers and events of life, they impact these three parts of a human being. How a person handles these three characteristics of themselves causes the person to exhibit one of the two types of behaviors: react or respond. If the person's body is not in the

right condition because of chemical imbalance, unhealthy nerves, the impact of the five senses (sight, smell, hearing, taste, and touch), which cause interpretation of the brain, sleep/ eat or exercise, and the impact of street drugs and alcoholic drinking, Then~~THEN~~ **these elements of the body influence the soul elements (mind, emotions, and will) and the beliefs in the heart which results the person to react or respond in their behaviors.**

The goal of my book is to assist the reader by discovering the correct process for making informed and wise decisions.

This Therapist wants to present the **three concentric circles**: the inner circle is the Spirit, the middle circle is the Soul, and the outer circle is the Body. See the attached diagram.

3 Concentric Circles

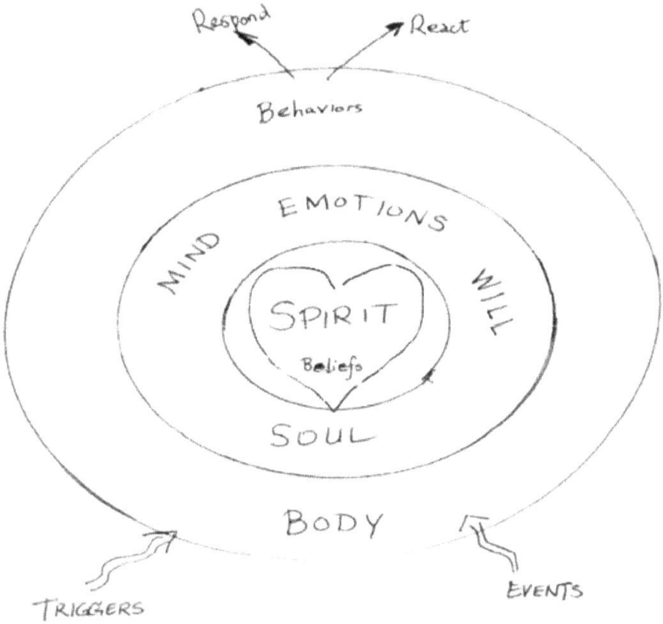

OUR DECISIONS DETERMINE OUR DESTINY

Thomas Monson, 2005

TABLE OF CONTENTS – 17 STEPS

1. **PRESENT THE 3 CONCENTRIC CIRCLES --- Body, Soul, Spirit**
2. **HOW TO DEAL WITH STRESS OF LIFE'S TRIGGERS AND EVENTS that causes a person to REACT or RESPOND**
3. **SECTION 1 --- BODY: The Body qualities will impact and affect and influence a person's BEHAVIOR --- REACT VS. RESPOND**
4. **CHARACTERISTICS of the BODY that may contribute positively or negatively to a person's sanity – 5 SENSES, Chemical Imbalance, Organs, Cells, Nerves, and Brain**
5. **REACTIONS = PASSIVE, AGGRESSIVE, PASSIVE –AGGRESSIVE**
6. **SECTION 2 --- SOUL: (PERSONALITY)**

   The SOUL consists of 3 PARTS (see 3 Concentric Circles): MIND, EMOTIONS AND FREE WILL.
7. **MIND --- a Part of the Soul --- "CARNAL" or Secular MIND IS DOMINATED BY WHAT A PERSON CAN *SEE, TASTE, HEAR, SMELL,* and *FEEL.***

8. **EMOTIONS: a Part of the Soul - 4 BASIC EMOTIONS: MAD, SAD, GLAD, AFRAID**
9. **WILL --- a Part of the Soul -- The WILL consists of the Endocrine System, Immune System, and the Nerve System. The will is the faculty of choice by which a person determines their freedom of action.**
10. **<u>SECTION 3</u> - SPIRIT: IN THE HEART CONTAINS THE BELIEF SYSTEM**
    1.PURPOSE(AIM)
    2 MEANINGFUL(SIGNIFICANCE) 3. SELF-IMAGE(DIGNITY) **Beliefs affect behavior and can affect a person's presentation and shape his entire reality.**
11. **<u>SECTION 4</u> -- TRUTH = Truth introduced into life provides guidance, wisdom, strength, courage, motivates, comfort, and faith. Objective truth is absolutely regardless of our opinion, perceptions, and our understanding. - WHERE DO WE FIND OBJECTIVE TRUTH?**
12. **<u>SECTION 5</u> – *SPIRIT:* INTRODUCE WISE BELIEFS DEVELOPED FROM OBJECTIVE TRUTH to establish a solid Belief System that impacts the Soul**

13. **PRESENCE OF SPIRITUAL DECEPTION – influences the Soul & Body in 3 ways 1) COMMISSION 2) OMMISSION 3) DISPOSITION**
14. **SECTION 6 - *SOUL* ----- The SOUL consists of 3 PARTS. When the Soul agrees with the Spirit by aligning with the TRUTH, double-mindedness does not occur.**
15. **SECTION 7 - *BODY ----- FLESH (The Brain interprets perceptions of the ears, hands, eyes, or the five senses -- smell, taste, feel, see, hear)* "The mind governed by the flesh (Body) is demise but the mind governed by the Spirit is life and peace."**
16. **SECTION 8 - *BEHAVIORS* – When a person agrees with objective TRUTH, that person has become empowered/equipped with the Spirit to impart wisdom to the Soul, which in turn directs the Body to RESPOND, not React to life's events.**
17. **RESPOND = ASSERTIVE, POSITIVE, DECISIVE**

COMPREHENSIVE EXPLANATION AND UNDERSTANDING OF THE TABLE OF CONTENTS:

This author wants Each reader to understand the game plan & trajectory of the 17 steps outlined in the table of contents

This author introduces a person who is faced with life's events and triggers. This person listens to his body qualities in Steps 3 and 4, which brings about his reactions to deal with these triggers, step 5. This author wants to show that this is how most people handle life from the outside inward. As his brain in his body speaks to the soul, thereby demonstrating a secular mindset, step 7. It produces certain types of emotions to help him feel better, adjust, or cope with these triggers, step 8.

The third element of his soul, the Will, in step 9, incorporates what the body, the mind, and the emotions are configured to display his behavior and reactions to manage life. This person justifies his reactions comprised of his secular, selfish beliefs to shape his reality, step 10.

This author presents the concept of objective truth to this person to convince or persuade him to allow himself to accept a new trajectory to cope and manage new constructive behaviors in addressing life's events and triggers, step 11.

Step 12 encourages this person to listen to objective truth, which creates a belief system in his heart. When faced with life's triggers/ events, with this new disposition, this person does not listen to his body qualities but instead listens to the beliefs in his heart that impact his soul, step 12.

However, along the way, spiritual dynamics come into a person, step 13, to sway him to change his mind or let his emotions dictate his reactions so people will feel sorry for him, or he will manipulate situations for his selfishness.

This author informs this person to deflect the negative spiritual dynamics and conduct life from the inside out, not the outside inward. This person allows his Soul to agree with the Spirit by aligning with the Truth, step 14. He then conducts life with wise beliefs, sensible thoughts, and healthy emotions to control the body in step 15 and pronounces the will's intentions to respond, not react to life's events and triggers, in step 16.

Step 17 explains and elaborates on what Respond means and conveys.

DEFINITIONS OF THE 3 CONCENTRIC CIRCLES

The Spirit is the deepest foundation of a person, and a person's core BELIEFS have been developed by (nurture and nature) cultural, social, experiential, family/parental mandates, and trauma. It is where INTUITION "gut feeling," or "sixth sense," exists, which demonstrates the ability to understand something immediately without the need for conscious reasoning or government laws. Without societal laws, it is the gut feeling that something is just not quite right or the Belief that a person knows instinctively what is right and what is wrong without governmental laws, traditional mandates, or social pressure.

The Soul is made up of three more parts: the mind, the emotions, and the will. **First**, the mind is the cortex, the prefrontal cortex, which is the Decision part of the brain. **Second**, the emotions part of the Soul is the portion of the brain called the amygdala, which is the memory or history part of the brain. A person's responsibility is to move out of the emotional part of the brain, the amygdala, where they make unhealthy decisions in order to move to the cerebral cortex to make healthy decisions. **Third**, the will involves the immune, nervous, and endocrine systems to display healthy and productive behaviors within the body.

The Will is where a person exhibits or shows the manifestation of what a person is thinking or what a person is feeling at the time as the Will conveys the message to the Body.

The BODY appears as an instrument of the soul, for example, in acquiring knowledge or in executing decisions of the will, or it simply appears as an expression of the soul, e.g., in language, in gestures, in a smile, or in a tear. The Body is directed by the Spirit and Soul to present Behaviors, which is the way in which one acts or conducts oneself. A person presents two distinct types of Behaviors: REACT or RESPOND.

REACT is the negative emotional declaration of 1. Passive (flight or avoid conflict), 2. Aggressive (fight or verbally disrespect), or 3. Passive-Aggressive (store up complications & later explode like a pressure cooker).

RESPOND is to be assertive. What are the characteristics of ASSERTIVENESS? They are the qualities to set boundaries, negotiate compromise, talk through things, look at ways that we can figure this out, resolve, look at gaining more information, be willing to be influenced in a healthy and productive way, walk calm, to present secure confidence, to demonstrate healthy self-esteem, to offer positive ideas and suggestions, to disagree respectfully (to agree to disagree with mate or friend), to contribute to a societal cause, to say no without guilt, to demonstrate courtesy, to ask for clarity, to promote positive communication, to honor and respect Truth, to portray constructive action or testimony to our Beliefs in the Spirit.

Before we investigate the 3 Concentric Circles (see diagram), let's explore the psychological and physiological stress of life's triggers, tragedies, and events. Notice that "stress" is not the event or situation. It is the psychological or physical interpretation of the event.

LIFE'S TRIGGERS AND EVENTS (see diagram) **HOW TO DEAL WITH STRESS OF LIFE'S TRIGGERS AND EVENTS that causes a person to REACT or RESPOND**

HOW TO DEAL WITH STRESS

This Therapist recommends that you:

- **(SPIRIT): Try to eliminate the stressors**: It's not always possible to avoid a stressful situation or problem. Evaluate whether you can change the situation that is causing you psychological stress, perhaps by setting boundaries, dropping some responsibility, relaxing your expectations, or asking for guidance or assistance.
- **(SOUL): Embrace social support**: Some friends or family members may be good at listening and empathizing.

Others may help, like bringing over a home-cooked meal or providing child care. Just make sure your relationships stay in balance. A friend who requires support but never reciprocates may increase your anxiety. A strong social structure can improve RESPONSE to stress.

- **(SOUL): Meditate**: To get started, set aside five minutes in a quiet place to sit and breathe. Focus on the present moment; if stray thoughts intrude, acknowledge them and then let them go. Gently refocus and bring the attention back to the present moment. Don't judge yourself for any mental wavering.
- **(SOUL): Seek Pleasure**: When life gets overwhelming, people often drop their leisure activities first. But cutting yourself off from pleasure can be counterproductive. Even when time is tight, look for opportunities to do something for yourself, whether that means reading a novel, singing along to your favorite tunes, going to a football game, taking your dog for a walk, playing an instrument, or streaming your favorite comedy. Laughter can benefit both mental and physical health.
- **(SOUL): Reframe your thinking**: The cognitive behavioral therapy approach is the understanding that our thoughts influence our emotions, which in turn influence our behaviors. Reframing your thoughts about

a stressor can help manage your feelings, thus reducing psychological stress. Emphasizing: If you feel yourself spiraling into imagining worst-case scenarios, stop and bring every thought captive to obedience to Rightness. Set realistic expectations for yourself. Strive for acceptance of situations outside of your control.

- **(BODY): Seek good nutrition**: When confronted with a stressor, the central nervous system releases adrenaline and the hormone cortisol during chronic stress, which can cause fat and sugar cravings. Research also suggests that high cortisol combined with high sugar consumption causes fat around internal organs that is associated with cardiovascular diseases. A diet focused on a variety of nutrients can both protect health and provide more physical energy to deal with challenges. Just aim to consume a rainbow of fruits and vegetables as part of your daily diet. Avoid using substances such as alcohol or drugs to dampen the stress because substances do not solve the root of the problem and can have serious health effects.
- **(BODY): Relax your muscles**: Because psychological stress causes muscles to tense, headaches, backaches, and general fatigue. You need to incorporate stretches, exercise, massage, or warm baths, get in a comfortable position, and choose a muscle group to focus on. Inhale

and contract the muscles for 5 to 10 seconds, then exhale and release the muscles suddenly. Simply picture each muscle group one at a time and focus on relaxing that portion of the body.

- **(BODY): Protect your sleep:** Try to have a consistent sleep routine that allows time to wind down before lights out. Journaling and relaxing can help with insomnia. Also, avoid caffeine and alcohol in the late afternoon and evening. More importantly, actively move your body during the day to improve your sleep at night, especially for middle-aged and older adults.
- **(BODY): Get physical**: A brisk 30-minute walk or a dance session in your living room can directly combat stress. In one study, working adults who participated in moderate physical activity had half the perceived stress as working adults who did not participate in physical activity. Physical activity can cancel or reduce psychological stress.
- **(SPIRIT & SOUL): Seek help**: If you feel overwhelmed and self-help isn't helping, look for a psychologist or other mental health provider who can help you learn how to manage your stress effectively. The Professional can help you identify false beliefs, stinking thinking, unhealthy concepts of situations, or unhealthy behaviors that contribute to your stress and then develop an action plan to

change the stressors, change your mental interpretation, change your environment, and/or change your responses.

3 CONCENTRIC CIRCLES:

The goal of this author is to inform the reader that a person is possessed by 3 Characteristics: body, soul, and spirit. See the Diagram. This author wants to present the outer circle – the Body.

3 Concentric Circles

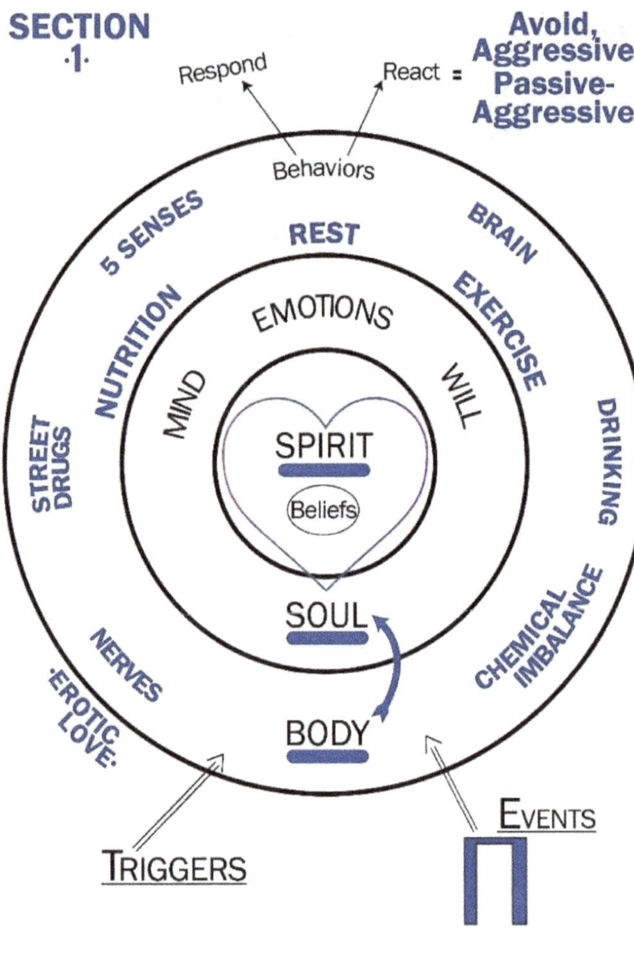

SECTION # 1

BODY: **(Physical Trajectory) : The Body qualities will impact and affect and influence a person's BEHAVIOR --- REACT**

Why is the health of the average American... plummeting?

Why are digestive issues like bloating, cramps, and constipation at the highest levels ever recorded?

Why do so many of us struggle with fatigue and low mood?

Why are skin problems, achy joints, allergies, and constant colds something that millions of Americans deal with every single day?

Why are 66% of Americans overweight, diabetic, or prediabetic…

And why is that number SKYROCKETING every day… with projections that in 10 years, a staggering **85% of all Americans** will be overweight or obese?

Why do so many people fill their bodies with drugs or drink to try to cope with insanity?

The characteristics of the BODY that may contribute negatively to a person's behaviors, sanity, self-actualization, wise decisions, and healthy emotional response are :

THE PRESENCE OF A PERSON'S BODY IS CONSTANTLY FACED WITH EXTERNAL TRIGGERS:

EVENTS, DILEMMAS, DIFFERENCES, HYPOCRISY, CONFUSION, DISTRESS, FLAGRANT, OBSTACLES, CHALLENGES, TEMPTATIONS, STRESS, CRAZINESS, SEXUAL ENTICEMENT, FLIRTING, CRITICAL, VERBAL ATTACK

THESE TRIGGERS IMPACT THE COMPONENTS OF THE BODY

BODY --- CHEMICAL IMBALANCES

Anxiety, ADD, ADHD, ASTHMA, Diabetes, High blood pressure, Hypertension, NEUROTRANSMITTERS like Serotonins & Dopamines, high Testosterone level, Estrogen level, Lymph nodes, Peptic Ulcer, Schizophrenia, and Hormone imbalance -- these imbalances create specific perceptions with the involvement of the above triggers to potentially live an unhappy life.

BODY -- - BRAIN

Interpret with senses, previous experiences, triggers from the nerves, Diet, Exercise, Substance Abuse, Sleep Quality, Cognitive Decline, and Injuries -- most people analyze the above triggers with these elements of the brain that cause people to react to triggers. This presents their reality.

BODY --- 5 SENSES

SIGHT, SMELL, HEARING, TASTE, TOUCH -- the above Triggers can influence these 5 senses to ignore what a person believes is right and cause stinking thinking

BODY --- NERVES, DNA

Impulses of muscles or organs, bundles of fibers that send and receive messages between the body and the brain, nervous agitation or irritability, heart rate dysfunction, blood pressure, irregular temperature, bladder problems, headaches – sometimes this Counselor has to encourage my clients to seek medical health with these nerves to be able to use the 3 concentric circles in a productive way.

BODY --- LOVE --- SEXUALITY

Infidelity, watching Pornography, im-pure thoughts and drama, and morally wrong activities like flirting may at first seem fun and entertaining, but later in the big picture may result in sad or destructive outcomes or relationships.

BODY --- STREET DRUGS CONSUMED

Heroin, Cocaine, Methamphetamines, LSD, Hallucinogens, Marijuana (weed), Ecstasy, Ketamine, Crack. Many people believe the consumption of these drugs helps them to feel better, but their side effects eventually catch up in negative, impulsive consequences.

BODY --- ALCOHOL DRINKING CONSUMED

VODKA, BEER, WHISKEY, CLASSIC COCKTAILS, RUM, TEQUILA, and more are introduced with the hope of coping with the craziness of life. However, as a result, it causes a person to live in a fantasy world for a period of time. The alcohol does not actually fix the situation.

THESE COMPONENTS OF THE BODY ALONG WITH THE EXTERNAL TRIGGERS CAN AND DO INFLUENCE AND CONTRIBUTE TO REACTIVE BEHAVIORS (see the top of the 3 concentric circles diagram)

THIS AUTHOR SUGGESTS EXPLORING IN GREATER DETAIL THE BODY COMPONENTS

Testosterone is a sex hormone, and Estrogen is one powerful hormone that plays an important role in the body. These sexual chemicals, Testosterone and Estrogen levels, impact Neurotransmitters, which influence chemical balance and promote communication between brain cells. They are sometimes called the "happy hormones" because of their function as mood and emotion regulators.

Men = Testosterone

Testosterone is a sex hormone that plays an important role in the body. In men, it's thought to regulate sex drive (libido), bone mass, fat distribution, muscle mass and strength, and the production of red blood cells and sperm.

Excessive levels of testosterone in men may be associated with hyperandrogenism, higher risk of heart failure, increased mortality in men with prostate cancer, male pattern baldness, criminality, impulsivity - (Impulsive actions are typically "poorly conceived, prematurely expressed, unduly risky, or inappropriate to the situation that often results in undesirable consequences. When such actions have positive outcomes, they tend not to be seen as signs of impulsivity but as indicators of boldness, quickness, spontaneity, courageousness, or unconventionality) and hypersexuality.

Ref: Wikipedia

Men with high testosterone can experience a variety of troubling symptoms: it can lead to more aggressive and irritable behavior, more acne and oily skin, worse sleep apnea, an increase in muscle, a lower sperm count, infertility, and shrunken testicles.

If you don't treat your high testosterone levels it can result testicular or adrenal tumors. It can raise your bad cholesterol levels, and it can thus lead to potentially resulting in a heart attack, cardiovascular disease, or stroke, and self-centered ways and a perspective different than women.

Ref: everlywell.com

Women = Estrogen

Hormones that are out of whack can wreak havoc, causing hot flashes, vaginal dryness, and similarly uncomfortable conditions. Estrogen is one powerful hormone. To keep your body and brain healthy, it's essential that your estrogen levels are balanced. If estrogen levels drop, your risk for heart disease goes up. Estrogen plays a major role in heart health. Estrogen boosts the production of the brain chemical serotonin. Serotonin balances your mood. That's why, when estrogen levels drop, in postpartum or menopause, many women suffer from depression. Estrogen is responsible for the development of your reproductive system. The anatomy of your vagina and uterus is dependent on this busy hormone. If hormones are out of whack, it can evoke victimization and perspectives different than men.

Dopamine or serotonin levels in the Body affect mental health conditions.

1). Serotonin deficiencies can impact mood, sexual desire and function, appetite, sleep, memory and learning, temperature regulation, social behavior, cardiovascular system, and muscles. Dopamine deficiency can cause medical conditions like Parkinson's disease, restless leg syndrome, depression, schizophrenia, and ADHD. 2). Neurotransmitters affect the electrical activity in the **Brain** (in the Body), which in turn influences the MIND (in the Soul).

OXYTOCIN = Stronger Bond between Partners

When a couple has SEX, it releases Oxytocin, a bonding chemical, so the more sex with your mate, the stronger the bond. Ladies, some men have a chemical imbalance of diabetes, cholesterol, or ADHD. Other men have a chemical imbalance of their serotonin and dopamine, which requires more physical touch in order to activate the outcome of the Oxytocin chemical in the body to affect their mental state in a positive way. However, if the partners fail to collaborate together as one or one of the partners chooses not to address this deficiency, then there will be complications and confrontation among them, and they must seek professional counseling.

ADD / ADHD = Involves problems with focus and concentration. A person with this deficiency may have a hard time following a conversation because their attention is jumping all over the place. People with ADD are often highly intelligent folks, but this deficiency impacts the mind and the emotions in the soul, causing a person to occasionally lack the ability to focus or be late for appointments.

OCD = This deficiency requires prescribed meds to positively alter compulsive behavior, agitation, compulsive hoarding, hypervigilance, impulsivity, repetitive movements, ritualistic behavior, social isolation, or persistent repetition of words or actions.

MOOD = For Clinicians -- Mood disorder primarily affects the **Brain** in the body. Neuroimaging techniques like FMRI can show chemical imbalances in neurotransmitters of the Brain. This condition in the brain located in the body with these characteristics: Cyclothymia, hypomania, major depression, dysregulation, and bipolar, which impacts the Amygdala located in the soul with these characteristics: anxiety, apprehension, feelings of worthlessness, sadness, guilt, phobia, or panic attack.

THE REASON TO EXPLORE IN GREATER DETAIL THE (above) BODY COMPONENTS is to show how the deficiencies in Body chemistry can impact the mental strength of a person triggered by life's triggers. The Reader should seek professional counseling to address the issues and be held accountable with respect to the components.

INTRODUCTION OF LEGAL DRUGS in the Body will demonstrate healthy or unhealthy outcomes. Let's look at one of many drugs.

Magnesium – the natural "chill pill"

Magnesium is often referred to as a relaxation mineral. It has been called the natural "chill pill."

In the brain, magnesium helps regulate the receptors that play a critical role in learning, memory, and mood. Without sufficient magnesium, these receptors become hyper-excitable, causing brain cells to become overstimulated. This neuronal dysfunction caused by a lack of magnesium can also lead to both mood disorders and problems with the ability to focus and make decisions.

A study investigating the potential benefit of magnesium supplementation in women who were suffering from frequent emotional stress found that at baseline, the majority of women were suffering from symptoms like irritability, fatigue, and sleep disorders, and 60% presented magnesium deficiency.

INTRODUCE ALCOHOL

Most people claim they introduce Alcohol to Cope with Life's Triggers and Life's Events. Some folks innocently declare that Drinking and Drugs are social delicacies to engage in with others. Over time, the long-term risk of alcohol can lead to high blood pressure, heart disease, stroke, liver disease, and digestive problems. So, in turn, will these long-term risks influence the soul and affect reactions?

If this is true, then why would individuals engage in alcohol or beer consumption? Most of my couple clients come to me with this issue and wonder why they are having relationship challenges.

Some of my clients will express they know the answer to a better life:

"Yeah, I drink too much beer/ liquor/ alcohol. OK, I'll stop drinking, and everything will be better, and my relationship with my wife will improve." The attempt to transform the self from the outside circle (Body) to the inner circle (Spirit) fails to achieve solid transformation.

With respect to your life goals, it is necessary to determine how life controversies, life challenges, trauma, victimization, and more impact the Body.

SEE THE DIAGRAM - we are faced with **life events or life circumstances**, tragedies, and traumas that affect our bodies. The Body's qualities will impact, affect, and influence a person's BEHAVIOR.

Let's explore the results and outcomes of the Body with Actions and Behaviors addressing life events and circumstances.

BEHAVIORS of the BODY

Two types of Behavior are: 1. REACTIONS and 2. RESPONSES.

These two words, **react or respond**, are foundational to how we demonstrate healthy mental processing.

What is characterized as healthy **responses** and unhealthy **reactions**? Focus is placed on allowing ourselves to experience our natural emotional **reactions.**

REACTION – **defined:** it is an act in reply to something. For instance, you hit me, so I'm going to hit you. You annoyed me, so I will get my revenge. You yelled at me, so I will yell back. The partner's reaction is a reverse movement or tendency or an action in a reverse direction or manner. Reactions are done on impulse, without putting much thought into it or considering what the end result may be.

REACTIONS = there are three types of reactions:

- PASSIVE--(FLIGHT) (Gottman says STONE-walling),
- AGGRESSIVE--(FIGHT) (Gottman says CRITICAL),
- PASSIVE –AGGRESSIVE--(FRIGHT) (Gottman says DEFENSIVE-ness, CONTEMPT).

First Example: The wife complains that her Husband criticizes her for not moving on past his violation of Infidelity. She complains that her Husband gets defensive when they try to talk about why he violated their covenant. She shares that the Husband holds her in contempt because she spends too much money and does not give him the love he deserves. She complains that sometimes the Husband avoids a fight and commits stonewalling, so she admits to trouble sleeping and the need to take meds to help her. Do you see the four types of Reactions committed by the Husband?

Second Example: Regarding one of my clients, he shared that he leaves work and stops by the bar to get a drink of **Vodka to calm him** from his busy day at work and to gain the strength from the drink to face his demanding wife when he arrives home. This Client is showing his Reactions to ease his tension of life's events with work and to prep for life's trigger of his demanding wife by using the coping skill of drinking.

This Therapist instructs the couple that a serious change must be made, so it is imperative to find new coping skills rather than using a strong drink to deal with life. Discovering those wiser coping skills **calls for digging deeper into the soul and spirit** to reveal motives, intent, and stinking thinking.

Third Example: For you Clinicians -- **From a more strict Clinical / Mental Health diagnosis -- ANTI-SOCIAL PERSONALITY DISORDER:**

(See Reactions here and later under Spirit capture the Core Beliefs)

Diagnostic Criteria

At least three out of seven characteristics

1. Failure to conform to social norms regarding lawful behaviors; Repeatedly performing acts that are grounds for arrest

2. Deceitfulness: lying or conning others for personal profit or pleasure

3. Impulsivity or failure to plan ahead

4. Irritability and aggressiveness: repeated physical fights or assaults

5. Reckless disregard for the safety of self or others

6. Consistent irresponsibility; failure to honor work or financial obligations

7. Lack of remorse; indifference to or rationalizing harming others

Fourth Example: More serious reactions:

1. Lust – the pursuit of sexual/ sensual desires in a selfish way
2. Gluttony --- is a person using food consumption as a way to cope with life
3. Greed --- mental focus on self-gratification
4. Sloth –self-centered ego with laziness, little motivation, and little positive desires
5. Wrath - serious anger expressed with a desire to punish someone, sometimes in violent ways
6. Envy – selfish desire for something that another person has; similar to jealousy
7. Pride – overbearing, haughty, arrogant superiority over other people

Go with this author on a journey through the body and the processing steps (Spirit and Soul) that lead us to react to life or to respond to life (Behaviors in the Body).

If the person's body is not in the right condition because of chemical imbalance, unhealthy nerves, the impact of the five senses (sight, smell, hearing, taste, and touch), which cause interpretation of the brain, sleep/ eat or exercise, and the impact of street drugs and alcoholic drinking, THEN these elements of the body influence the soul elements

(mind, emotions, and will) and the beliefs in the heart which results in the person to react in their behaviors.

SOUL IS THE CONNECTOR BETWEEN THE BODY AND THE SPIRIT --

- resilience
- optimism
- self-esteem
- meaning and purpose
- having positive relationships
- a sense of accomplishment
- emotional stability
- experiencing positive emotions
- vitality: feeling energetic.

***The transition from Body to Soul: CONSCIOUSNESS* --- Attitude**

Attitudes are thought to have three components: an affective component (feelings), a behavioral component (the effect of the attitude on behavior), and a cognitive component (belief and knowledge). Attitude is a position of the body properly derived from the Soul's three parts. So, for the reader, this author wants to present the 2nd Concentric Circle.

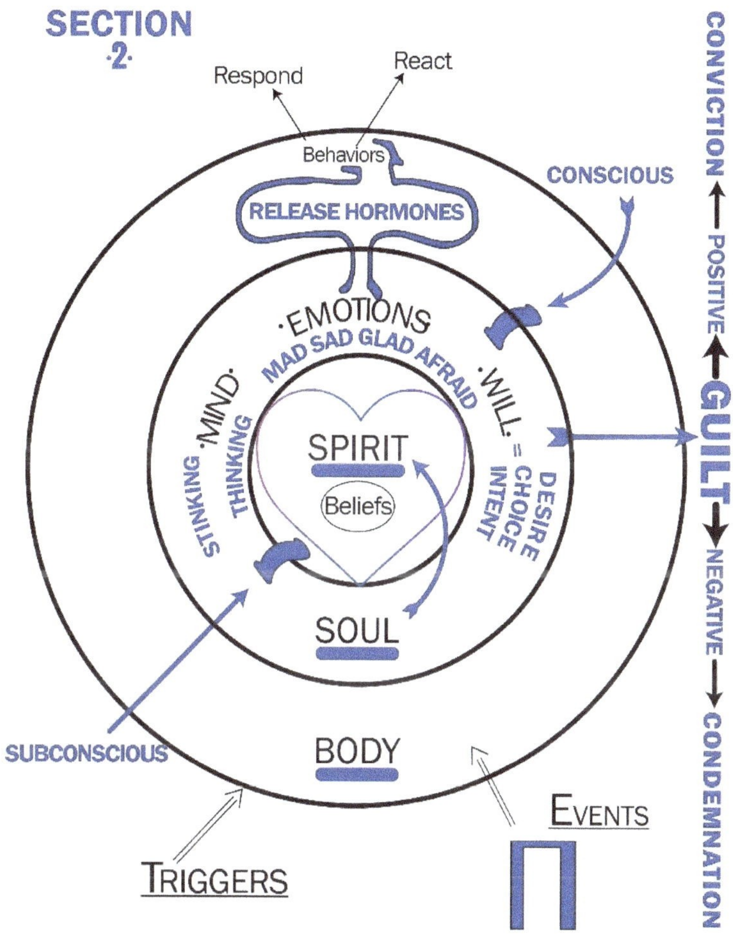
SECTION
·2·
Respond
React
Behaviors
RELEASE HORMONES
CONSCIOUS
·EMOTIONS
MAD SAD GLAD AFRAID
·MIND·
THINKING
STINKING
·WILL· = DESIRE
CHOICE
INTENT
SPIRIT
Beliefs
SOUL
BODY
SUBCONSCIOUS
TRIGGERS
EVENTS
CONVICTION
POSITIVE
GUILT
NEGATIVE
CONDEMNATION

SECTION # 2

SOUL: (PERSONALITY)

1. Insecurity 2. Inadequacy 3. Inferiority 4. Co-Dependent 5. CONFIDENCE 6. INFLUENCE 7. RESPECT 8. FREE WILL 9. MEMORY 10. PERCEPTION

Our soul is our personality: who we are. Our soul's purpose is why we are here on this earth at this time. What we are looking for or seeking is probably connected to our soul's purpose. It is an aspect of our life that drives and moves us forward.

With the influence of contemporary society, the soul thinks, reasons, considers, remembers, and wonders as the mind embraces the five senses influenced by the brain. In the Soul, we experience emotions like anger, compassion, happiness, love, relief, and sorrow, which causes each person to let emotions dictate reacting behaviors (see the Feeling Wheel on page 37). There are only four basic Feelings: MAD, SAD, GLAD, and AFRAID. Then, by activating the Will in the Soul, we are empowered to show intent, motivation, resolve, choice, and desires toward behaviors.

This author wants to present that these characteristics are not created by this therapist, but as you can see, they were developed long ago before this therapist.

THE SOUL HAVING THREE PARTS according to History

1. AQUINAS

Aristotle's thought taken over by St. Thomas Aquinas:

The transcendence of the spirit over material reality (body) is manifested by the immateriality of thinking; this means that the soul, having an activity that is intrinsically independent of material conditions, cannot have a mode of being inferior to its mode of acting (body). In other words, it must be essentially independent of matter.

Does the human soul really enjoy the type of superiority over the body that this ontological interpretation implies? Does experience not show that man's spiritual soul is dependent upon his body in many ways? Man comes into being through biological conception and birth; the very existence of his soul seems thus to be conditioned by his body. And what about fatigue, illness, and death? In all these cases, is the soul not subject to the law of the body? How can one bring such arguments in harmony with Thomas's conception of a soul that exists in its own right, in ontological independence of the body?

The main thing to be noted about these experiences, however, whether they be positive or negative, is that the Thomas explanation does not conceive these as an interplay between two realities but rather a mutual conditioning of two constitutive principles in one reality: the soul is conditioned by the body, just as the body is conditioned by the soul.

2. CATHOLIC: Is the soul dependent upon the body and/ or vice versa?

The **relationship between body and soul has been a topic of discussion** for centuries. According to the Catholic Encyclopedia, the body is a real and essential part of man's nature, but not in such a way that the soul is essentially subjected to it or ontologically dependent upon it.

The soul does not participate in the existence of the body, but the body is assumed in the existence of the soul. Thus, although body and soul really coincide in man's substantial unity and in total mutual conditioning, there is a one-way dependence in the strict sense of the word, namely, that of the body upon the soul.

3. PLATO

Plato defines the soul's three parts as the logical part, the spirited part, and the appetitive part.

The first part of the tripartite soul is:

Logistikon

This is the part of the soul that loves logic, thought, and rational learning. Plato equated this part of the soul with those who refrain to a high degree from doing harm to another. They actively assist one another and generously support their community.

Thymoeides

According to Plato, the second part of the soul is called thymoeides, and this is usually thought of as the most spirited of the three parts. It is this part of the soul that causes people to experience strong emotions of mad, sad, glad, and afraid.

Epithymetikon

Finally, the third part of Plato's soul was called epithymetikon, and this is thought of as the appetitive part. It is the part of the human soul that cannot resist appetites, including those for food, power, and sex. This part of the soul is often conflated with the Freudian id.

In Plato's view, epithymetikon existed in opposition to the soul's other two parts; he considered desire to be ultimately illogical. He thought that the major tasks of the soul's other two parts included working tirelessly to resist the appetitive (Will) part.

Several other historical Philosophers share their concepts of the Soul:

Delitszch held that the soul was a sort of efflux of the spirit, the link between the spirit and body. He asserts that the soul and spirit are of the same nature but of different substances, ((whatever that may mean)). The spirit has the threefold power of willing, thinking, and expressing; the soul is the doxa of the spirit and has a sevenfold manifestation.

Ellicott, Liddon, and others speak of soul and spirit as a lower and higher side of man's nature, having to do with different departments, the spirit being the region of the intellectual forces, the soul of feelings, affections, and impulses.

Heard's and others are much grosser and are illustrated in a very coarse way. **The soul is the enabling structure of the union between body and spirit.** The body's actions and the spirit combine to make a soul, just as oxygen and hydrogen combine to produce water. The soul midway between the body and spirit at first was in a state of equilibrium; it might either incline to the demand of the body or to the spirit.

This author wants to bring the wisdom from these historical, philosophical leaders to our contemporary culture. These attributes and characteristics presented in

history did not become permanent mental and physical healthcare concepts. This author is going to show all readers the benefits of understanding the functions of these attributes and characteristics to transform lives that historic philosophy leaders presented.

Soul contains 3 Parts:

Soul= Thoughts (Mind)+ Feelings (Amygdala) + Free will (Temporal)

Our soul acts as a valve between the spirit and the body.

The soul, credited with the ability to enliven the body, was located by ancient anatomists and philosophers in the lungs or heart, in the pineal gland (Descartes), and generally in the brain. The contemporary culture today stresses qualities to keep people happy with co-dependent characteristics, exhibiting selfishness with Narcissistic characteristics or obsessive-compulsive qualities to seek perfection. These qualities happen as a result of conditional love (Soul), not unconditional love (in the Spirit) with self or result from the family of origin dynamics, the conditional complexities in a covenant relationship, or the humanistic demands pushed onto people.

When making a decision, we form opinions and, involving a mixture of intuition and rational thinking, choose actions via mental processes that are influenced by biases, reason, emotions, and memories. The simple act of deciding supports the notion that we have free will. We will weigh the benefits and costs of our choice, and then we cope with the consequences. Factors that limit the ability to make good decisions: missing or incomplete information, urgent deadlines, and limited physical or emotional resources. All of the above qualities mentioned declare the Soul listens to the Brain. (See the 3 Concentric Circle Diagram from Step 1 Diagram, page xx).

3 Concentric Circles

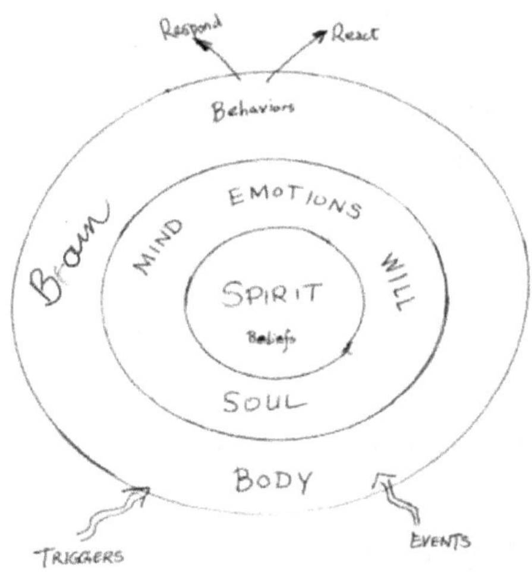

Soul= MIND (Thoughts)

Is this TRUTH?

Secular MIND IS DOMINATED BY WHAT A PERSON CAN SEE, SMELL, HEAR, TASTE, AND TOUCH INTERPRETED BY THE BRAIN.

This author declares there is more to life than making decisions based on these elements --- so let's explore.

A. Diligent pursuit of being HAPPY. In our contemporary culture, happiness is generally considered a positive state of mind. People seek the release of the feel-good chemicals in the brain. Yet, there are so many unhappy people.

B. Have you ever tried to push away a negative thought only to feel it grow stronger? There's a saying — "What you resist, persists." — This is **PEACEKEEPING**. Avoiding or Ignoring stress or conflicts between partners or difficult situations is what all my clients were doing when they started therapy. This therapist asked the client, how is that working for you?

C. Your MIND is different than your Brain.

The BRAIN controls a person's movements and various bodily functions and is dominated by the five senses. Animals have brains, but humans have brains and minds. The MIND is the frontal lobe of the Brain, which contributes to a person's morality, reasoning, intelligence, and understanding.

BRAIN (BODY)

The cerebral hemisphere can be subdivided into four lobes, each associated with different functions.

Together, the lobes serve many conscious and unconscious functions, such as body movement, processing information from the five senses, interpreting language, intelligence, and personality.

The largest lobe of the cerebral cortex is the frontal lobe, located at the front of the brain behind the forehead.

This Cerebral cortex lobe, which is the outer surface of the brain, is associated with higher-level processes such as decision-making, conscious thought, problem-solving, aspiration, attention, consciousness, reasoning, language, and memory, which is the MIND.

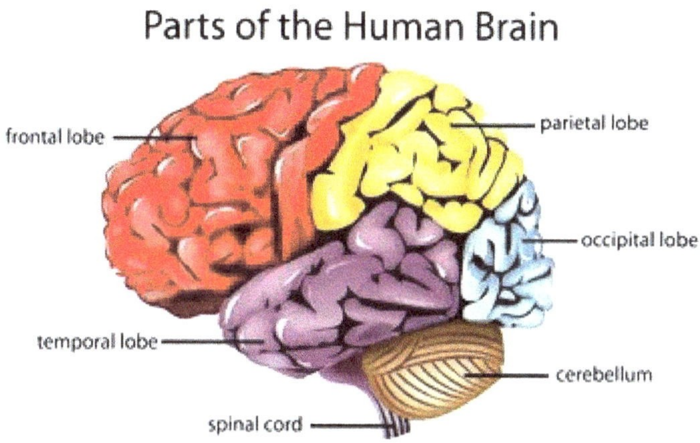

Secular Mind is dominated by the five senses.

Does the Brain (in the BODY) or the Mind (in the Soul) – Determine Sexuality?

We may be closer to understanding how it happens.

Posted June 11, 2017 on Psychology Today

MIND vs. BRAIN

Psychology Today – Article

Brain causes Gender to determine?

Testosterone, it appears, plays a major role in the development of sexuality. In the 1980s, when Germany was still divided into a Western segment and an Eastern one under

the domination of the Soviet Union, a group of Eastern scientists proposed that human homosexuality was the result of insufficient exposure to testosterone in the womb. Since the moral atmosphere of the time in that country regarded homosexuality with abhorrence, they proposed that all pregnant females should have the fluid surrounding their male fetuses tested for testosterone. Testosterone acts on the ***brain*** *by activating a complex protein – Androgen Receptor.*

Early excessive testosterone in XX (female) embryos – a condition called Congenital Adrenal Hypertrophy (CAH) – results in abnormally high amounts of testosterone in females. {The over-abundance of testosterone in females and the lack of testosterone in males can suggest that a person is a different sex type than the body the person lives in.}

Joe Herbert M.B, Ph.D.

Hormones and the Brain

Summary: So too much testosterone or estrogen in the body activates the brain (androgen receptor) to live life according to the five senses of the body: see, taste, hear, smell, and feel, which results in a REACT to facing life's triggers [see the Diagram] which becomes described as the Secular Mind.

This author would like to ask the reader to examine this group of people along with another group of people: sex addicts.

These two groups have a chemical imbalance, which, in the world of therapy, should be treated in the same manner. One group is mandated to come to see this therapist to help address and cope with this chemical imbalance, while the other group is allowed to continue to exist and be welcomed by the general public. These two groups that have a chemical imbalance are treated differently:

In one group, it's okay for a male who has a lot of estrogen in his body in order to like males or feel like a female, but in the other group, it's not okay for the male to have a lot of high serotonin and dopamine's in his body to act out his desire for women, to have multiple consenting relationships. It is a proven fact that these two groups, which have their unique chemical imbalance, do, in fact, impact and affect society's rules and regulations (Olympic competition) and also influence and impact Family, friends, and observers of these groups in their own unique negative way. However, in our current and contemporary society, one group is permitted to manifest and project its philosophy of life onto others. Meanwhile, the other group is mandated to engage in professional help mentally and medically to alter their philosophy of life. This author intended to keep each statement discreet so that the reader could reasonably and rationally discern and understand the point being presented.

The chemical imbalance of the two groups is nature and nurture, so why is it that those guys in one group can go off and be transvestites or guys-loving guys, while guys in the other group cannot have multiple consensual girlfriends or wives. THEREFORE, the Brain in the body with a chemical imbalance impacts the development of sexuality presentations. Whereby these two groups should seek out assistance from a medical doctor to incorporate meds to address the chemical imbalance, learn to live wiser than the five senses of the body, and seek help from a professional counselor to dig deeper into their SOUL and SPIRIT to transform their mindset to present a reasonable, responsible member of society.

D. Mental Health trends: Victim

A person's mental health is shaped by life's events: social engagements, economic and environmental conditions, along with body issues like genetics. To improve mental health within society at large, we need to address the social determinants of poor mental health, including poverty, economic insecurity, unemployment, low education, social disadvantage, homelessness, and social isolation. These determinants can trigger a person to feel like a victim.

VICTIM – a person who allows toxic thoughts, blame and shame of self or others, or feeling harmed, or more psychological stress that grows developing mental illness and creates physical illness.

E. Secular Mind: Plato's Logistikon portion of the Soul conveys the rationale and logic to result in wise decisions, good community members, and demonstrating confidence and strong self-esteem, but because of the influx of selfish ways, victim mindset, or people pleasing can cause the loss of these qualities.

F. SERIOUS Violations:

1. Lust – the pursuit of sexual/ sensual desires in a selfish way
2. Gluttony --- is a person using food consumption as a way to cope with life
3. Greed --- mental focus on self-gratification
4. Sloth – represents a lack of required/ necessary action
5. Wrath – Strong vengeful anger with a desire to punish someone
6. Envy – resentful & unhappy because someone else possesses what one wishes himself to possess
7. Pride -- Driven by an inflated sense of self-reliance

Another group to examine that exemplifies a popular selfish mindset:

ANTISOCIAL PERSONALITY DISORDER:

(See the Reactions under Section 1 and capture the Beliefs under Section 3)

MAJOR COGNITIVE ERRORS

Mind Reading

Minimizing

Excuse-Making

Blaming

Extreme Optimism

Intellectualizing

Justifying

Rationalizing

MIND: MENTAL WELLBEING:

Are Mental illness and mental health two sides of the same coin?

Mental health and mental illness are not simply two sides of the same coin. Mental health, just like physical health, demonstrates characteristics and qualities from weakness to strength.

Someone living with a mental illness can be experiencing optimal mental health at any point in time, while someone else can feel sad or frustrated even in the absence of a mental illness.

With physical health, some days we naturally feel stronger and more energetic than others. Similarly, some days, our mental health is worse than others, and that, too, is a natural part of being human. We may feel tired, grumpy, sad, angry, anxious, depressed, stressed, or even happy at any point in time. These are all normal human emotions and aren't on their own a sign of mental illness.

Differentiating between poor mental health and symptoms of a mental illness is not always clear-cut. When poor mental health has a sustained negative impact on someone's ability to work, have meaningful relationships, and fulfill day-to-day tasks, it could be a sign of mental illness requiring treatment.

The absolute cure of mental illness and transformation toward solid mental health can happen by opening up to a new philosophy of life, presented in the later portion of this book.

The following now is the presentation of 5 characteristics to keep a person in check to use these skills to promote and/ or sustain mental health.

How can a person stabilize mental health?

Incorporating the following five qualities will help you feel more positive. The principles presented later in this Book will reveal the ultimate mental health.

1. Connect with other people

Good relationships contribute to mental well-being. They can:

- build a sense of self-worth and integrity with the unconditional love belief incorporated
- give an opportunity to share the journey of life together with positive mental choices
- with the truth of empathy, provide emotional support, and allow you to support others

2. Be physically active

Being active is not only great for your physical health and fitness. Evidence also shows it can also improve your mental wellbeing by:

- raising your self-esteem
- helping you to set goals or challenges and experience satisfaction in achieving the goals
- causing chemical changes in your brain, which can help to positively change your stinking thinking

3. Learn new skills

Research shows that learning new skills can also improve your mental wellbeing by:

- boosting self-confidence
- incorporating communication skills or strategic goals to build a purpose-filled life
- embrace forgiveness and commit to wiping the slate clean mentally

4. Give to others

Research suggests that acts of giving and kindness can help improve mental wellbeing by:

- creating positive feelings and a sense of satisfaction and reward
- giving a feeling of purpose and self-worth
- helping to connect with other people

It could be small acts of kindness towards other people or larger ones like volunteering in your local community.

5. Pay attention to the present (mindfulness)

Paying more attention to one's current lifestyle can improve a person's mental well-being. This includes thoughts, feelings, brain perception, and the five senses of the body, as well as the handling of life's triggers and events.

Some people call this awareness "mindfulness". Mindfulness can help a person be more content and positive when faced with obstacles and challenges. Also, it can help a person understand themselves better. The latter half of this Book will demonstrate how to activate Mindfulness.

Soul= + EMOTIONS(Amygdala)

According to Plato, the second part of the soul is called **Thymoeides**, and this is usually thought of as the most spirited of the three parts. This author expands on Plato's concepts with more specific descriptions of only four categories of basic emotions.

4 BASIC EMOTIONS: MAD, SAD, GLAD, AFRAID

SEE THE FEELING WHEEL

(Glad = Peaceful, Powerful, Joyful)

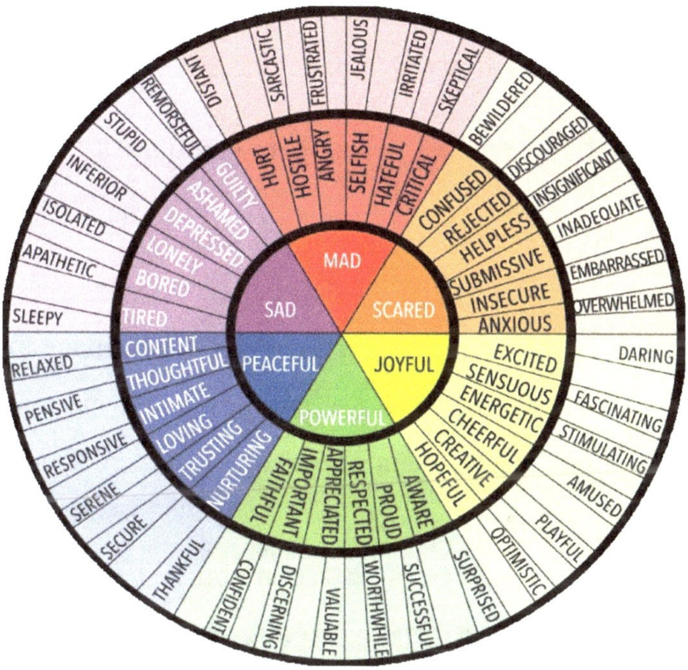

EMOTIONS:

AMYGDALA - a **region of the brain primarily associated with emotional processes**. The name amygdala is derived from the Greek word amygdale, meaning "almond," owing to the structure's almond-like shape. The amygdala is located in the medial temporal lobe, just anterior to (in front of) the hippocampus in the brain, which **helps regulate emotion and encode memories**—especially when it comes to more emotional remembrances. AMYGDALA releases hormones into the body to affect, impact, and influence will and behaviors. Many of my clients have demonstrated that emotions have framed and caused certain types of REACTIONS.

The following are a few examples of Emotions:

A. **Happy:** Why can't you be happy? Happy is an emotion. Many people struggle with happiness because of stress, being too hard on themselves, living in the past, holding grudges, walking in fear, and many more.
B. **Guilt, Blame, Shame:** I beat myself up every day - trying to forgive myself every day! Second, the underlying sense of not being a good person; and third, the negative feeling that arises out of the injustice perceived in the world.
C. **PTSD:** Disasters, Tragedies, or sudden overwhelming incidents bring about what is called Trauma, which results in sleepless nights, overthinking, or depression.

The absolute cure of solid mental health and emotional strength can happen by opening up to a new philosophy of life, presented in the later portion of this book.

Soul= + Free WILL

The third part of Plato's soul was called **epithymetikon**, and this is thought of as the appetitive part.

The third part of the soul is the will. It is best described with the following questions: what are my intentions? What's my desire? What's my preference? That's the temporal lobe part of the brain, which connects all of it in order to display a wise decision with our behaviors.

These Nouns describe the essence of the WILL:

1. Cravings 2. Urges 3. Decisions 4. Moral conviction 5. Morally enslaved 6. Desires 7. Affections 8. Vows 9. Loyalty 10. Selfishness 11. Dedicate 12. Trust 13. Respect 14. Forgive 15. Determine 16. Promote 17. Reconcile 18. Perspective 19. Lead 20. Follow 21. Obedience 22. Declare 23. Restore 24. Trajectory

The WILL consists of the Endocrine System, Immune System, and the Nerve System.

ENDOCRINE SYSTEM: This System contains 40 million brain cells influenced either directly or indirectly by serotonin related to mood, sexual desire and function, appetite, sleep, memory and learning, temperature regulation, social behavior, cardiovascular system, muscles, and various elements in the endocrine system.

IMMUNE SYSTEM: The system works to root out germs and other invaders.

NERVE SYSTEM: The nerve system has fibers that carry important messages back and forth between the body and the spirit, as well as the spinal cord. It tells your heart to beat and your lungs to breathe. It controls the way you move and your five senses in the body.

Ref: WebMD

These three systems are influenced by the subjective TRUTH, thoughts, and emotions a person embraces, which display mostly reactions to life's encounters.

Story # 1: Regarding one of my clients, he shared that he leaves work and stops by the bar to get a drink of Vodka to calm him from his busy day at work and to gain the strength from the drink to face his demanding wife when he arrives home. This Client is showing his Reactions to ease his tension of life's events with work and to prep for life's trigger, whereby he perceives a demanding wife.

So, addressing the three parts of the Soul with this Client:

First, the Client's mind is dominated by the brain's interpretation of the five senses in the Body. Second, the Client's emotional disposition of being mad from his thoughts (mind) of work and facing his wife triggers his reaction (body) to exhibit

14 Forgive 15. Determine 16 Promote the characteristic of being passive-aggressive. Third, the combination of the thoughts in his mind and the emotions in his amygdala causes his desire (will) to consume the Vodka after work.

Association Areas of Brain

The association areas are spread throughout the cerebral cortex in the four lobes. These areas act by integrating information from these brain regions, often adding more complexity to their functions.

These association areas can also form connections to sensory and motor areas to give meaning to and organize information in these areas. **Association areas** within the frontal lobes are involved in key processes such as planning, thinking, and feeling.

These areas also play a role in personality and controlling emotional behaviors. Association areas within the parietal lobe are involved in spatial skills such as spatial awareness and reasoning, as well as being responsible for paying attention to visual stimuli in the environment.

In **the temporal lobes**, association areas function primarily in memory processes, such as helping to process procedural and episodic memories. These areas also communicate with other lobes of the cortex so they can complete memory-related processes.

Occipital lobe association areas help to facilitate memories associated with visuals to be retained, as well as enable us to think in a visual manner.

A well-summarized description of the human SOUL is: Our soul is our personality, who we are. With our soul, we think, reason, consider, remember, and wonder. We experience emotions like guilt, happiness, love, shame, sorrow, anger, fear, relief, and compassion. And the Will helps to resolve, choose, and make decisions. So, the essence of the human soul activates the subconscious.

This author's objective is to assist readers who are looking for ways to improve their self-actualization relations with others and to convert their behavior reactions to healthy responses.

The absolute cure of the three components of the Soul (mind, emotions, will) by opening up to a new philosophy of life will be presented in the later portion of this book to bring about a fresh new life.

TRANSITION from Soul to Spirit: SUBCONSCIOUSNESS

Subconsciousness is the bridge between spirit and soul that notices and remembers information when you're not actively trying to do so, and it influences your thoughts or behavior even though you don't fully realize it. For this transition, this author wants to present the 3rd Concentric Circle.

SECTION
·3·

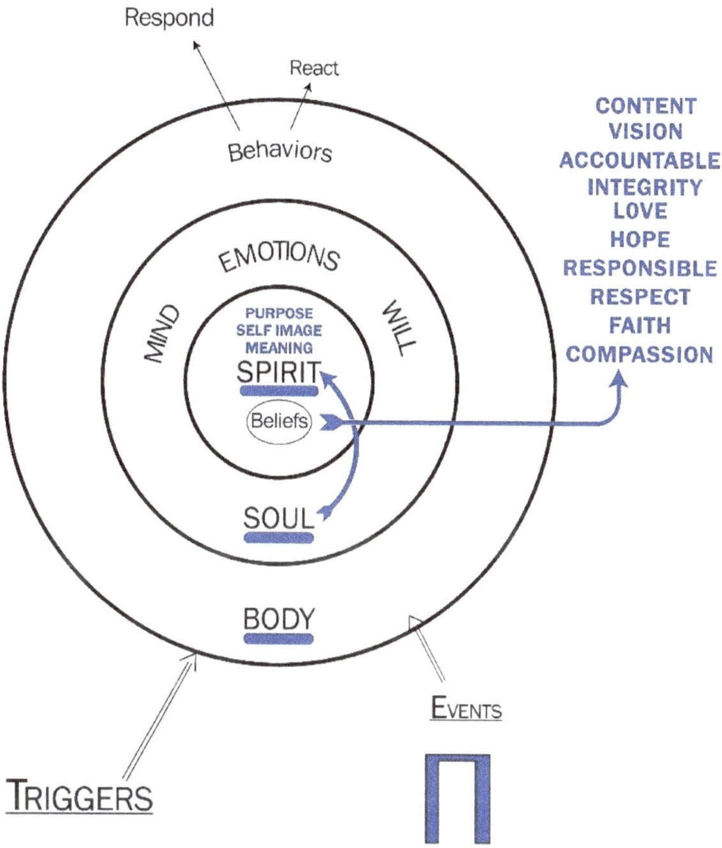
Respond
React
Behaviors
EMOTIONS
MIND
WILL
PURPOSE
SELF IMAGE
MEANING
SPIRIT
Beliefs
SOUL
BODY
CONTENT
VISION
ACCOUNTABLE
INTEGRITY
LOVE
HOPE
RESPONSIBLE
RESPECT
FAITH
COMPASSION
EVENTS
TRIGGERS

SECTION # 3

SPIRIT = IN THE HEART contains the BELIEF SYSTEM

BELIEF SYSTEM = Beliefs affect behavior and can affect your life and shape your entire reality.

Belief System is a set of values, morals, principles, and worthiness to direct a person to understand these 3 Elements of a Belief System:

1. PURPOSE (Aim) 2. MEANINGFUL (Significance) 3. SELF-IMAGE (Dignity)

Most people don't realize that their spirit is the core of their being. They function mostly out of their soul realm, believing what they think and feel is reality. But what they think and feel, based upon the five senses of the body, is their perception. Their perception becomes their reality.

THE FIRST ELEMENT IN THE HEART:

1. PURPOSE

AIM: (See the Diagram) The "subjective" TRUTH a person chooses to embrace in their Spirit creates a belief system that sets challenging mental health, selfish ways, an appearance of a stable disposition, prompts of unhealthy course / or path for a person's life.

Readers, let's explore the AIM in your heart. What Beliefs develop your Purpose and decision-making?

WHAT ARE YOUR CORE BELIEFS?

The following are practical values, morals, principles having foremost importance:

Reader, take this opportunity to write down your definition or Wikipedia's definition of these concepts.

- Integrity: ______________________________
- Responsibility: __________________________
- Respect: others __________________________
- Kindness: _______________________________
- Tolerance: ______________________________
- Courtesy – say PLEASE and THANK YOU. ________
- Self-Discipline __________________________
- Accountability: __________________________
- PEACE: _________________________________
- Perseverance: ___________________________
- Discipline: ______________________________

- Compassion: Being kind or ______________________
- Cooperation: __________________________________
- Hope: ______________________________________
- Love: ______________________________________
- JOY and Happiness: ___________________________
- Faith: ______________________________________
- Forgiveness: __________________________________
- Health and Fitness: ____________________________
- Honesty/ Truth: ______________________________
- Positive Attitude: _____________________________
- Money – handling: _____________________________

Your behaviors influence your beliefs, showing your PURPOSE or (Aim)

SCENARIOS ABOUT HOW A PERSON EMBRACES SECULAR OR WORLDLY TRUTH, WHICH IMPACTS BELIEFS (in the Spirit) TO AFFECT SELFISH THINKING, SELF-CENTERED EMOTIONS, AND REACTS TO CIRCUMSTANCES NOT RESPOND TO CIRCUMSTANCES:

SCENARIO #1 SUBSTANCE ABUSE --- Regarding one of my clients, he shared that he leaves work and stops by the bar to get a drink of Vodka to calm him from his busy day at work and to gain the strength from the drink to face his demanding wife when he arrives home. This Client is showing his Reactions with a drink to ease the tension of life's events with work and to prepare for the trigger of his demanding wife, which conveys his secular Belief system.

So, addressing the three parts of the Soul with this Client:

First, the Client's mind is dominated by the brain's interpretation of the five senses in the Body. Second, the Client's emotional disposition of being mad from his thoughts of work and facing his wife triggers his reaction (body) to exhibit the characteristic of being passive-aggressive. Third, the combination of the thoughts in his mind and the emotions in his amygdala causes his desire (will) to consume the Vodka after work.

SCENARIO #2 SQUEAKY WHEEL GETS THE GREASE --- Why does a person raise his voice with a harsh tone? He has learned from watching others that the squeaky wheel gets the grease. He feels like he's not being heard, so raising his voice will mean that others will hear him better and that his desires will be met. So, in his soul, he has developed these thoughts of the squeaky wheel getting the grease from his brain interpreting the five senses. So, as a result, he operates out of his soul.

SCENARIO # 3 WORLDLY TRUTH IMPACTS SELFISH BELIEFS ---- The Client has said that he had no part in the demise of his three previous marriages. He did nothing wrong in any of them and declares he doesn't carry any baggage from the previous marriages into his current relationship.

There are some people who believe that their past relationships do not impact their current relationship situation. Unbeknownst to this gentleman, he has conveyed a **belief.** If this person has truly not made peace with his past and put the past where it belongs - in the past, then this person's belief can cause some stinky thinking and cause him to react to present life's events as so noted by his present spouse.

THE SECOND ELEMENT IN THE HEART =

2. MEANINGFUL SELFISH BELIEF: Please see how the Behaviors (in the Body) impact the Beliefs (in the Spirit) that cause people to embrace worldwide Truth. This Truth influences how a person makes decisions, which results in reacting and not responding to life's triggers.

SELFISH BELIEFS have also been called FALSE Beliefs:

A false belief is an idea that you live by. In fact, it most likely causes you a tremendous amount of stress.

PRINCIPLES: We often form these self (false) beliefs as a survival tactic:

1. The world is fair, and if I try hard, I will succeed.

2. The world owes me a living.

3. If my partner is that way, then I have to let him be, so I choose to disconnect. My mate should want to change for himself and not for me to please me. If he is changing his character to please me, then he is manipulating me.

4. If I treat people well, they will always treat me well.

5. My environment determines my state of mind.

6. "If I grew up in a loving, supportive family, I would be a loving, supportive person." "If I grew up in a dysfunctional family, then I am destined to fail in relationships."

7. My emotional state depends on the actions of my spouse.

8. "In a troubled marriage, I have only two options—resigning myself to a life of misery or getting out of the marriage." *Thousands of people live in self-made prisons because they believe in this myth of limited choices. Do not let yourself believe that you have only two options in a desperate marriage. Don't simply settle for misery or divorce.*

9. "Some situations are hopeless—and my situation is one of these." *The person who accepts this myth believes: Perhaps there is hope for others, but my marriage is hopeless. The hurt is too deep. The damage is irreversible. There is no hope.*

10. You don't have to ask for a raise because your boss will recognize your worth and give you one.

11. If you exercise enough, you will lose weight, even if you have a few beers.

12. Everything will work out in the end.

13. Separation makes the heart grow fonder.

14. "I can't tell the truth because I may get judged…"

15. "I don't want to get close to this person lest my heart gets broken…"

16. "I can't trust people because I've been betrayed too many times before…"

17. "I can't pursue my dreams because I don't know what I'd do if I fail…"

18. Smoking weed or drinking Vodka helps me to calm down and deal with life.

19. I believe that if I think about life without my partner because I'm unhappy … then life will be better.

20. "get get get .... materialism - everything on earth is all there is. We love things and use people." Reader, can you identify with any of these BELIEFS presented?

SCENARIO # 4 EMPHASIS ON BELIEFS: When a person experiences trauma, he may develop beliefs that the world is unsafe and unpredictable. Then, most book authors do not continue to emphasize the concept of beliefs. This author wants to address the issue of beliefs strictly, specifically, and with great detail and emphasis. Many of us simply convey what appears as our thoughts, but when we are challenged, encouraged, or when we make an effort to look much deeper into these thoughts, they convey beliefs that we then operate.

BELIEF: For example, why did the client commit infidelity? ... to send a firm message to his wife?

1). ALCOHOL: The Client consumed alcohol, which became a trigger to open the door to inappropriate behaviors (body) like infidelity to communicate a message to his spouse. What is this Client's Belief that converts into a thought?

2). The client and co-workers were at a Training out of town at a Hotel. The female co-worker asked the Client to stay in her hotel room for the evening to talk. She said the Client was easy to talk to. She was learning skills for a new job and wanted to talk about her day. She was drunk. She started kissing the Client. The Client felt a moment of relief. He shared that this encounter felt nice ---- all the problems were gone, exploring a new adventure. At that time, the Client was not sure what he wanted. Because this event occurred with a co-worker, the Client was unsure about staying married to his wife.

3). The client had previous experience with this female co-worker at work. He kissed her on three different occasions and was not caught or confronted by anyone. He saw he could get away with it. He felt too comfortable with her for the last incident. She asked the Client to stay because he was easy to talk with. Also, because they were out of town and out of the office at a hotel, no one would discover his encounter with this female co-worker. The client encountered sex with her since he got away with these intimate moments the3 times before. This Therapist took the opportunity to show how his BELIEF was formed because he had not experienced consequences with the other 3 times before. This Therapist presented the three concentric circles (see diagram) and showed him how his belief in getting away with the encounters with the female co-worker shaped his thoughts and feelings on this last encounter and caused his will to set his behaviors to go further with sexual intimate encounters with this girl. So, this is why the Client committed the Infidelity and now is troubled by the guilt, shame, and pain of hurting his wife.

THE THIRD ELEMENT IN THE HEART =

3. SELF-IMAGE (Dignity)

Your beliefs may impact your self-actualization.

Health and disease are influenced by multiple interacting factors, many of which are not fully under a person's control, including genetics, exposure to environmental toxins, history of trauma, and socioeconomic circumstances. Beliefs impact a person's dignity by shaping their own self-worth. For example, middle-aged adults who held more positive beliefs about aging lived an average of 7.6 years longer than those who held more negative beliefs, even when controlling for current health and other risk factors.

As a licensed Therapist, I work with all sorts of individuals diagnosed with Mood and Personality Disorders. One group of folks I assist is those diagnosed with SELF-IMAGE called Narcissism. The beliefs of a Narcissist are the root cause of this disorder.

SCENARIO # 5 ***Narcissistic Personality Disorder*** (NPD) is one of 10 personality disorders presented in the fifth edition of the *Diagnostic and Statistical Manual of Mental Disorders* (DSM-5), the Industry standards we counselors are required to follow. The dominant signs of NPD include an inflated sense of self-importance, a lack of empathy for others, and a deep need for constant attention or admiration. NPD's self-esteem can be super fragile, dependent on external validation, or self-deception. Narcissism exists on a spectrum: On one side, it's craving the occasional compliment. On its darkest side, it can creep into pathological territory.

They'll believe grandiose fantasies about themselves (i.e., they're smarter, more attractive, and more successful than everyone they know), easily put other people down, and generally hijack any conversation or situation to make themselves feel better or superior. Feeling "less than perfect" is very uncomfortable for a narcissist, and they'll protect themselves from it at all costs. The individual lacks good insight into what's going on. The Narcissist thinks that the problem is all about everyone else, not them. For a Narcissist, it starts with what they **BELIEVE**!

A personality disorder like NPD is about disturbed relationships: they have a lifetime of struggles with intimate, interpersonal relationships with their family, friends, and co-workers.

Differences for Men and Women with NPD The disorder affects anywhere from 0.5% to 5% of the general US population, with a greater prevalence in men than women.

The percentage is low because someone with NPD has to admit they have issues—which they often don't. And it can manifest differently in men versus women. According to research, compared to males, a narcissistic female personality is more likely to include deep insecurity, martyrdom, jealousy, and competitiveness with other women. Men, on the other hand, are more likely than women to exploit others, feel entitled to certain privileges, and exhibit qualities of assertiveness or the hunger for power. However, this is not to say these traits are exclusive to either sex. When it comes to vanity and self-absorption, both sexes rate equally.

SCENARIO # 6 -- SELF-IMAGE Carol's story of INSECURITY (the name is changed to comply with HIPPA) As I was working with Carol recently, she expressed concern that her husband has changed. From her perspective, she indicates that he seems to not have as much interest in her now, married almost 30 years. She has come to therapy to work on herself. She conveys to me that she feels she's no longer pretty because of her gray hair and the change in her body contour. She states that she is insecure about herself and her looks.

She believes she is not attractive. See the Concentric diagram. The client did not realize that her thoughts were actually her beliefs. She said no one has ever shown her that in the past. This therapist showed her that our beliefs become the truth for which we live. With respect to this client, the truth became evident that her beauty was her loyalty to her husband, her sensitivity to his perspective, and the external issue that her husband, over the years, has declined in his mental strength. The client began to see that her beliefs direct her thoughts, which impact her behaviors. This therapist showed the client that she must change the way she believes about her beauty.

SCENARIO # 7 SELF-IMAGE Counseling sessions with Dave (the name is changed to comply with HIPPA) He was troubled because his wife's illness is serious, and if his wife dies, then he will need to care for her four children and his family does not want Dave to neglect his biological daughter. He is concerned about his BELIEF, which is that one day, the kids may not see him as their father. The neglect of his daughter will make him angry that he tried to be a father to his biological and stepchildren together.

This discussion caused this Therapist to bring out the 3 CONCENTRIC CIRCLES. His BELIEF of stepchildren in the future may cause him to act and make decisions today in a certain way. Today, these stepchildren see Dave as their dad.

This Client shares about his biological dad, who took responsibility for his stepsisters. This Therapist challenged the Client to ask his bio father if years ago his father questioned his role to be a father to children and stepchildren and from what he BELIEVED that he did or did not ponder to be a father to all the kids. The father accepted his SELF-IMAGE of fatherhood, which demonstrated a BELIEF.

This Therapist brought to light the 3 CONCENTRIC circles that his deep BELIEFS of insecurity of the current situation or the future are impacting his thoughts, feelings, and his will to React, not Respond. His fear of failure to raise children and stepchildren causes the Client to miss his Purpose and his Aim for his positive qualities.

Beliefs about your basic character—who you are as a person on a fundamental level—can be especially powerful. Research suggests that while Guilt (feeling that you did a bad thing) can motivate a response to self-improvement, Shame (feeling like you are a bad person) can tend to create a Reaction of a self-fulfilling prophecy, which can reduce hope and undermine efforts to change. The Truth is that you are a Human Being inside and are a Human-Doing on the outside. Your belief in Truth can influence your Dignity.

Your beliefs influence other people's behavior.

Your beliefs can shape your reality not only by influencing your own behavior but also by influencing other people's behavior, from close relationship partners to complete strangers. In one classic study, male participants were led to believe that a woman with whom they spoke on the phone was either attractive or unattractive. Analysis of the recordings by outside observers showed that throughout the conversation, women perceived as more attractive came to behave in a more friendly and likable way than those who were perceived as less attractive, suggesting that participants' expectations not only shaped their own perceptions of their conversation partner—they also seemed to elicit behavior that confirmed their expectations. This phenomenon has been demonstrated in a number of other contexts as well, including interactions between teachers and students.

Your beliefs may also elicit corresponding behavior from romantic partners. Research suggests that people who see their partners in a more **idealized light** than their partners see themselves tend to become more satisfied with their relationships over time, experience less conflict, and are more likely to stay together. Why might this be? One explanation is that idealizers instill confidence in their partners and alleviate their partners' insecurities about the relationship. More secure partners are, in turn, more likely to behave in generous and constructive ways, fostering greater relationship satisfaction. By contrast, those who over-perceive hostile intentions in their partners during conflicts are more likely to behave in ways that elicit the very hostility and rejection they fear. This author will present concepts in the latter half of this book for partners to embrace the **"idealized light"** of their partner.

OBSESSIVE COMPULSIVE DISORDER: Beliefs

Another Personality Disorder this Therapist works with is Obsessive-Compulsive Disorder, which is intrusive, distressing, and causes anxiety. I simply want to offer a brief overview of the general components that help keep OCD going.

A good place to start is by learning about two **beliefs** that are common in many people with OCD:

- **Inflated responsibility** – a belief that they are responsible for preventing harm or diligently working to bring happiness to a loved one or others so they will feel loved
- **Overestimation of threat** – a belief that things are riskier than they are

For someone with OCD, whatever intrusive thoughts they have seems very likely to happen, and their sense of responsibility means that they feel they must act in order to control the craziness. In other words, the two beliefs create an ever-increasing cycle of obsessions and compulsions. Even if the obsessive thoughts regarding the level of danger are assessed to be low by the person with OCD, their heightened sense of responsibility dictates the need to carry out a compulsion.

OCD is driven by the fear of consequences, no matter how unlikely they are. For someone with OCD, the perceived level of risk is turned on its head; a 0.01% risk feels as likely to happen as a 99.9% risk. **This conveys the belief system.**

ANTISOCIAL PERSONALITY DISORDER: BELIEF SYSTEM

REMEMBER the Reactions described under Section 1 Reactions and now capture the Core Beliefs

Exclusive Trait: Exploitation

Most Important Deficiency: Honor

Fundamental Pattern: Violations

View of Themselves: Superior

View of Others: Suckers

View of the World: Dog-Eat-Dog

Deals with the World by: Opportunism

Typically Comes Across as Callous

How can beliefs affect behavior?

Beliefs Affect behavior in the following ways:

- **Limiting beliefs limits people's potential: Limiting beliefs** affects behavior by preventing people from taking certain actions that they would have otherwise taken if the correct belief was there.
- **Beliefs and information filtering:** Just as I said before, we filter information based on our beliefs and only absorb the information that matches our belief system. This impacts our behavior by making us biased toward what we believe in, no matter how much proof is provided. That's why **persuading someone** to believe in something against his beliefs is hard.
- **Beliefs shape reality:** If a guy thinks that he will never **find a job** (a belief), then he will not become motivated to prepare himself for the job market (change in behavior), and later on, when he tries to find a job he will fail (so his belief will become true).
- **Beliefs and self-confidence:** Self-confidence is no more than a set of beliefs that you have about yourself. If those beliefs were positive, then you would behave like a confident person, while if they became negative, your behavior would be changed to the opposite. That's how beliefs can shape reality.

How the relationship between behavior and beliefs can be useful

It is now clear that beliefs can control your actions, behavior, and potential. If you learn how to acquire positive beliefs and how to get rid of negative ones, then you will be able to use the tremendous power of constructive beliefs on your side. The power of constructive beliefs comes from the truth a person hears, receives, and makes public. Stay tuned so you can discover those constructive beliefs from Objective Truth.

The goal of this author is to inform the reader that a person is possessed by 3 Characteristics: body, soul, and spirit. When a person is confronted with the triggers and events of life, they impact these three parts of a human being. How a person handles these three characteristics of themselves causes the person to exhibit one of the two types of behaviors: react or respond. If the person's body is not in the right condition because of chemical imbalance, unhealthy nerves, the impact of the five senses (sight, smell, hearing, taste, and touch), which cause interpretation of the brain, sleep/ eat or exercise, and the impact of street drugs and alcoholic drinking, THEN these elements of the body influence the soul elements (mind, emotions, and will) and the beliefs in the

heart which results in the person to react or respond in their behaviors.

<u>The goal of this book</u> is to assist the reader in understanding how individuals process information while influenced by their own personal perspectives to arrive at decisions that affect positive, neutral, or negative outcomes. Observe the three concentric circles diagram. This author wants the reader to discover the reactions and responses, which are the two types of behaviors manifested. Take the journey to see the behaviors of reacting or responding that evolve from the free will in the soul. The will, consisting of the endocrine, nerve, and immune systems, gather manifestations of the emotions derived from the Amygdala and the thoughts created by the mind, not the Brain. The mind and the emotions in the soul are impacted by the beliefs in the depth of a person's spirit.

Transformation must now take place to reject subjective truth and embrace objective truth for the purpose of converting from unproductive beliefs to productive beliefs to respond, not react, to life's triggers. So, let's explore objective truth.

SECTION ·4·

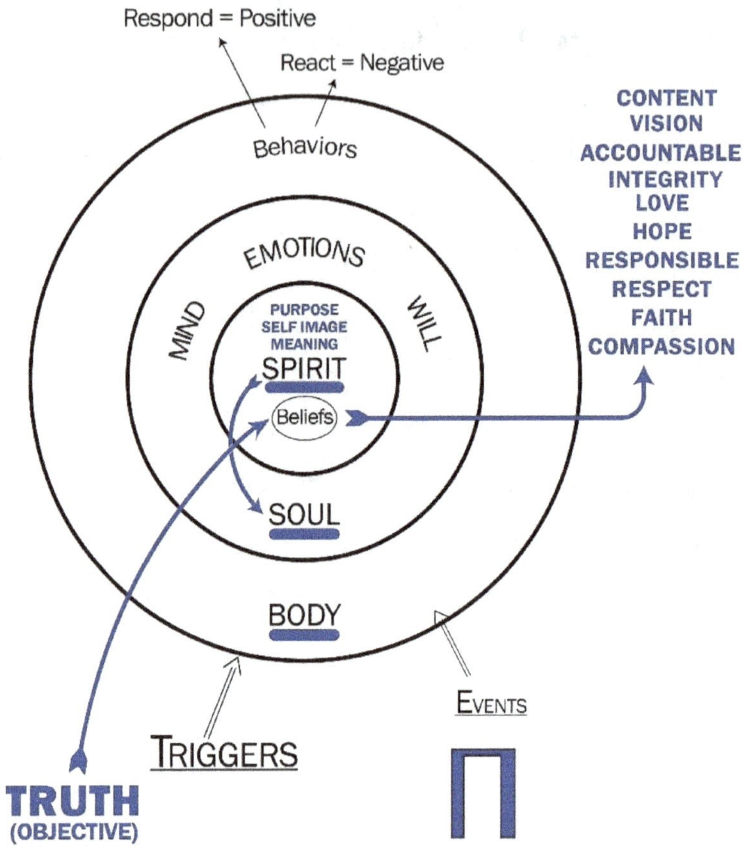
Respond = Positive
React = Negative
Behaviors
EMOTIONS
MIND
WILL
PURPOSE
SELF IMAGE
MEANING
SPIRIT
Beliefs
SOUL
BODY
CONTENT
VISION
ACCOUNTABLE
INTEGRITY
LOVE
HOPE
RESPONSIBLE
RESPECT
FAITH
COMPASSION
EVENTS
TRIGGERS
TRUTH
(OBJECTIVE)

That's why persuading someone to believe in something against his belief is hard

SECTION # 4

TRUTH = Truth introduced in life provides guidance, wisdom, strength, courage, motivation, comfort, and faith. Objective truth is grounded in substantial, unwavering principles and absolutely regardless of our opinions, perceptions, and our understanding. Where do we find OBJECTIVE TRUTH?

Is Truth based on your perception? Is Truth based upon societal rules, laws, rituals, or popular thinking? Is Truth based on our experiences to set us on a certain course?

Most people operate out of subjective truth, which is a property of beliefs, assertions, thoughts, and propositions in which people make certain decisions. It is for those persons who identify with sections 2 and section 3 of this book.

This author wants to promote a much broader and deeper description and explanation of the subject of TRUTH.

TRUTH IS THE BASIS AND FOUNDATION OF HOW PEOPLE SHOULD ACT, HOW PEOPLE SHOULD MAKE

DECISIONS, HEALTHY SELF-IMAGE, AND HAVE HEALTHY RELATIONS WITH OTHERS.

PURPOSE in a person's heart is the embracing of Objective Truth to be trustworthy, reliable, and believable.

There are different types of truth:

1. **Alethic:** Alethic Relativism asserts that truth is relative and that feelings overshadow facts.
2. **Agnostics**: Agnostics assert that it is impossible to know how the universe was created, so each person decides for themselves.
3. **Atheists:** Atheists base their value on science, pursue personal passion, and determine their own moral ethics.
4. **Holy Scripture:** Holy Scripture contains absolute truth by a Creator that, even challenged, remains unchanged and true for all people and groups at all times. There exists more external proof of the remarkable accuracy and relevance of the truths in Scripture than any other philosophical ~~truee~~truth.
5. **Moral Relativism**: Moral Relativism encompasses the differences in moral judgments among people groups cultures, and centuries.

6. **Secular mindset:** Secular mindset conveys freedom of belief in self-actualization, self-image, and self-centeredness, and there is no discrimination on the grounds of religion.

This objective truth provides protection in our decisions and in our relationships with others.

CLIMAX of TRUTH: UNDERSTANDING the concepts of SPIRIT, SOUL, AND BODY UNLOCKS THE SPIRITUAL REALM TO INVITE THE Objective **TRUTH** (see the 3 Concentric Circles diagram)

What is TRUTH in light of Life's Triggers & Circumstances?

This Concept can be seen most clearly in marriage. The bad outweighs the good:

Men decide to end their relationships when there are more times that they're fighting than having fun. When the bad times outweigh the good ones, most men think it's time to call it quits. Why stay in a relationship that makes you miserable? This is a perspective and an opinion (Subjective Truth), but it is not the OBJECTIVE TRUTH of a promise made between partners in the everlasting covenant.

What is the objective truth upon which you base your life? You have the right and are entitled to embrace the truth that you believe works best for you and your loved ones. You may be very passionate about certain truths. So, how is that working for you?

The perception of reality in your SOUL is secondary to the OBJECTIVE TRUTH of life that is captured in your core, the Spirit.

SO NOW IT IS IMPERATIVE TO EVALUATE AND INJECT CHANGE

I want to encourage you to keep reading because if you do these things, you will find it difficult to do it in your own power and in your own wisdom. I want to introduce you to concepts beyond our perceptions where you can gain more strength, power, and wisdom based on truth, not worldly popularity.

Where do we find OBJECTIVE TRUTH?

Transformation: We don't start from the outside and work inward of the Concentric circles. Instead, we start from the inside and work out to the Body - Behaviors.

SECTION
·5·

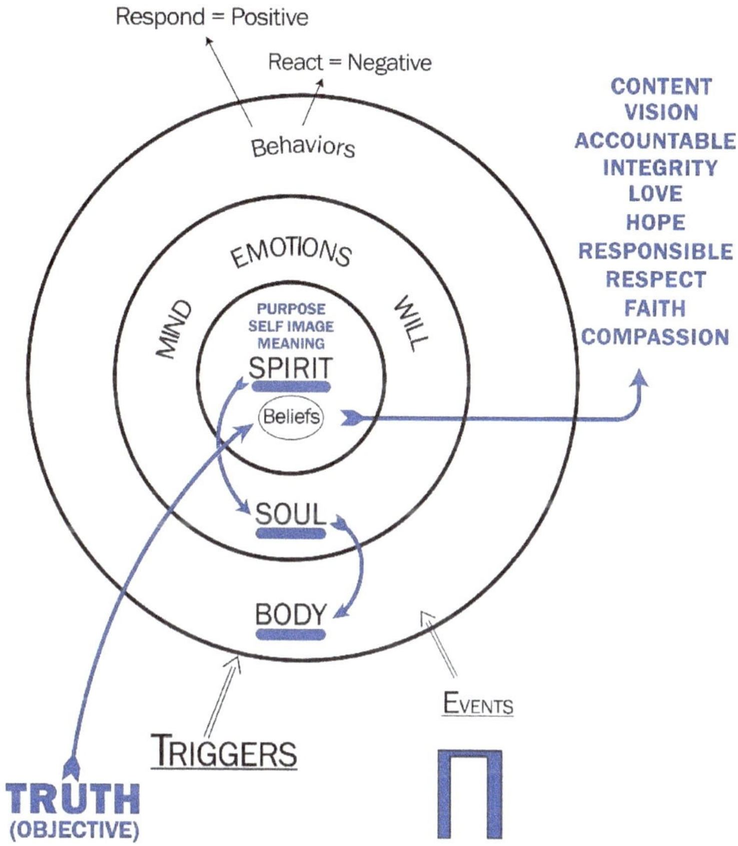
Respond = Positive
React = Negative
Behaviors
EMOTIONS
MIND
WILL
PURPOSE
SELF IMAGE
MEANING
SPIRIT
Beliefs
SOUL
BODY
CONTENT
VISION
ACCOUNTABLE
INTEGRITY
LOVE
HOPE
RESPONSIBLE
RESPECT
FAITH
COMPASSION
EVENTS
TRIGGERS
TRUTH
(OBJECTIVE)

SECTION # 5

SPIRIT: INTRODUCE WISE BELIEFS DEVELOPED FROM OBJECTIVE TRUTH to establish a solid Belief System that impacts the Soul positively

Belief System is a set of values, morals, principles, and worthiness to direct a person to understand these 3 Elements:

1. PURPOSE (Aim) 2. MEANINGFUL (Significance) 3. SELF-IMAGE (Dignity)

Transformation must now take place to reject subjective truth and embrace objective truth for the purpose of converting from unproductive beliefs to productive beliefs.

A person's perception becomes their reality.

1. Purpose:

When you know your purpose, you are content with your life. Content is much more satisfying and essential than the state of simple happiness.

AIM: (See the Diagram) The "subjective" TRUTH a person chooses to embrace in their Spirit creates a belief system of selfish ways. This author wants to introduce an Objective Truth that has worked for millions of people. You have probably heard this concept in pieces and in passionate presentations. I ask that you remain open-minded and receptive to hearing this complete Truth before you make your decision to accept or reject it.

Observe the 3 Concentric Circles diagram as you read the following.

"Those who live according to the flesh (BODY) have their minds set on what the flesh desires (my happiness, equality in marriage, selfish demands are met by others); but those who live in accordance with the SPIRIT have their minds set on what the Spirit desires (unconditional love, hope, and peacemaker not a peacekeeper)" (Romans 8:5) "So I say, walk by the SPIRIT and you will not gratify the desires of the Flesh. For the flesh (BODY) desires what is contrary to the Spirit, and the Spirit what is contrary to the flesh (BODY). They are in conflict with each other, so you are not to do whatever you want." (Galatians 5: 16-17).

AS THE FIRST STEP (See the 3 Concentric Circles diagram)

when a person opens their heart to this TRUTH, the Creator, in his mercy, regenerates a person's spirit through new spiritual birth, which happens at the moment when the person receives and believes in the raising of Jesus from physical death. (John 3:5--, 1 Peter 1). In this new birth, God's own life (i.e., the Holy Spirit) is added to a person's spirit, confirming and welcoming the person into the family of God. When the person heard the word of TRUTH, that person was marked with a seal, the promised Holy Spirit, generating inheritance (Ephesians 1:13). This new birth is also the fulfillment of God's promise, "I will give you a new heart and put a new spirit in you" (Ezekiel 36:26, NIV).

"For those who are led by the spirit of God are the children of God. The Spirit you received does not make you slaves so that you live in fear; rather, the Spirit you received brought about your adoption." (Romans 8:14-15 NIV)

"You were taught, with regard to your former way of life, to put off your old self, which is being corrupted by its deceitful desires; to be made new in the attitude of your minds; and to put on the new self, created to be like God in true righteousness and holiness."(Ephesians 4:22-24 NIV) So when a person embraces the truth of the gospel, that person is empowered by the Holy Spirit, which delivers extraordinary strength through the 17 attributes listed below.

The presence of the HOLY SPIRIT --- in a person's spirit:

1. Reveals the disposition of the Creator's heir -- Romans 8:15-18

2. Presents UNCONDITIONAL LOVE ----- 1 Corinthians 13: 4-7

3. Transforms the Mind -- Romans 12:2

4. Sheds light on one's inmost being -- Proverbs 20:27, 29

5. Promotes SELF-ACTUALIZATION — Hebrews 4:12

6. Plant TRUTH which can save from filth ----- James 1:21

7. Empowers with CONTENT in whatever circumstance -- - Philippians 4: 11

8. Empowered with extra-ordinary strength ---- Philippians 4:13

9. Urge Self-control --- Titus 2: 4 - 8

10. Presents Integrity --- Psalm 41:12

11. Clothed with Compassion --- Colossians 3:12

12. Give Hope --- Jeremiah 29:11

13. Express Sympathy and Empathy --- 1 Peter 3:8 – 9

14. Experience Peace --- Romans 8:6

15. Show Respect --- 1 Peter 2: 17

16. Bear with one another in Love --- Ephesians 4: 2

17. Be Accountable --- Hebrews 4:13, 16

Parents, wouldn't you feel like a successful parent when your children demonstrate and live these concepts in their lives every day?

So, the presence of the Holy Spirit in a person's spirit brings forth the working of and the benefits of God's Truth.

1. **THE TRUTH reveals STINKING THINKING – Blame, Guilt, People pleaser, Shame, Narcissism, Obsessive Compulsive, Avoidance, Critical, Contempt, Inadequate, Co-Dependent**
2. **Reasoning only goes to a limit --- so Faith in God's principles takes over = TRUTH.**
3. **Mind vs. Brain --- TRUTH impacts both but differently**
4. **Perspective differs – THE TRUTH revealed shows a person's bias. Truth reveals different perspectives among covenant partners.**

5. **Naturally Free – THE TRUTH can set a person free.**
6. **Decision–making - becomes wiser when it is based on TRUTH that is deeper and broader than Opinion.**
7. **Problem-solving – TRUTH gets you to the Cause.**

TRUTH - The mind controlled by the spirit is life and peace (Romans 8:6). Therefore, we have an obligation to live according to the spirit (Romans 8:12). The objective truth enlightens believers to empower embracing the following 21 Beliefs to radically transform stinking thinking.

21 BELIEFS: (See the 3 Concentric Circles diagram)

1. Obedience 2. Love 3. Forgive 4. Faith 5. Honor 6. Truth 7. Content 8. Strengths 9. Self-Control 10. Integrity 11. Compassion 12. Hope 13. Sympathy and Empathy 14. Peace 15. Respect 16. Tolerant 17. Accountable 18. Passion 19. Serve 20. Responsible 21. Kindness

Dear reader, the above 21 characteristics are much more fulfilling and satisfying than the pursuit of happiness. These are the characteristics that eventually affect Happiness. Also, on Page 10, Many of my addict clients thought life would improve if and when they stopped drinking and drugs. Real transformation does not happen from the outside inward.

Instead, healthy change happens from the inside outward. These 21 Beliefs in your Heart from the foundation of the truth, Scripture, Empower the drunkard, the addict, the narcissist, the Bipolar, and the drug user to conduct life in a fresh way.

WHAT ARE YOUR CORE BELIEFS FROM OBJECTIVE TRUTH?

The following are the practical values having foremost importance:

With respect to Scriptural truths, Readers take the privilege to record the positive qualities of Objective Truth.

- Integrity: (Proverbs 10:9 NIV) Whoever walks in integrity walks securely……
- Responsibility: (Galatians 6:4-5 AMP) Each person must carefully scrutinize his own work (examining his actions, attitudes, and behavior), and then he can have the personal satisfaction and inner joy of doing something commendable without comparing himself to another. For every person will have to bear with patience his own burden of faults and shortcomings for which he alone is responsible.
- Accountability: (Romans 14:10 - 12) …why do you treat your brother with contempt? ...So, each of us will give an account of ourselves to God.

- Respect: (1 Thessalonians 4:11-12 NIV) Make it your ambition to lead a quiet life. You should mind your own business and work with your own hands, just as we told you. So that your daily life may win the respect of outsiders and you will not be dependent on anybody.
- Kindness: (Galatians 5:22 - 23) Fruit of the Spirit is love, joy, peace, forbearance, kindness, goodness, faithfulness, gentleness, and self-control.
- Tolerance: (Ephesians 4:2) Be completely humble and gentle; be patient, bearing with one another in love.
- Courtesy: Always be ready to give an answer when someone asks you about your hope (Titus 3:2 CEB)
- Self-Control: (2 Timothy 1:7 AMP) For God did not give us a spirit of timidity or cowardice or fear, but he gave us a spirit of power and of love and of sound judgment and personal discipline (abilities that result in a calm, well-balanced mind, and self-control).
- PEACE: (John 14: 27 NIV) ____"my peace I give you" ______________________________
- Perseverance: (James 1:2-4 NIV) You know that the testing of your faith produces perseverance. Let perseverance finish its work so that you may be mature and complete, not lacking anything.
- Discipline: (Proverbs 19:20-21) Listen to advice and accept discipline, and at the end, you will be counted among the

wise. Many are the plans in a person's heart, but it is the Lord's purpose that prevails.

- Compassion: (Colossians 3:12) As God's chosen people, clothe yourselves with compassion
- Cooperation: (Philippians 1:5-6 NIV) I always pray with joy because of your partnership in the gospel from the first day until now, being confident of this, that God who began a good work in you will carry it on to completion.
- Hope: (Romans 15:13 AMP) May the God of hope fill you with all joy and peace in believing through the experience of your faith that by the power of the Holy Spirit, you will abound in hope and overflow with confidence in his promises.
- Love: Unconditional Love - (Psalm 44:23-26 NIV) Awake, Lord! Why do you sleep? Rouse yourself! Do not reject us forever. How do you hide your face and forget our misery and oppression? We are brought down to the dust; our bodies cling to the ground. Rise up and help us; rescue us because of your unfailing love.
- JOY, not happiness. Happy is about happening. Joy is inside. Happiness is on the outside. Joy becomes Content. Content leads to Gratitude. Gratitude reduces Grumpiness. Less Grumpy makes you…
- Faith: (Hebrews 11:1) Now faith is the confidence in what we hope for and assurance about what we do not see.

- Forgiveness: (Ephesians 4:31-32 NIV) Forgiveness is letting go of resentment, slander, and malice who hurt us. Forgiveness extends empathy, understanding, and compassion to others, which builds character and rebuilds self-esteem.
- Health and Fitness: (James 5:14-16 NIV) The prayer offered in faith will make the sick person well; the Lord will raise him up.
- Honesty/ Trustworthy: (Proverbs 12:19-22) Truthful lips endure forever, but a lying tone lasts only a moment. Those who promote peace have joy. The Lord detests lying lips, but he delights in people who are trustworthy.
- Positive Attitude: (Ephesians 4:22-24) "… to be made new in the attitude of your minds …"
- Money – (1 Timothy 6:9-10) Those who want to get rich fall into a trap and into many foolish and harmful desires that plunge people into ruin and destruction. For the love of money is the root of all kinds of evil. Some people, eager for money, have wandered from the faith and pierced themselves with many griefs.

Now, readers can compare the answers you wrote in section 3 to the values and principles shared from this objective truth, the Scriptures from our Lord. It is hard to live this life without the principles and extraordinary strength that come from our creator, Jehovah. These God-designed Beliefs bring about: 1. PURPOSE (Aim) 2. MEANINGFUL (Significance) 3. SELF-IMAGE (Dignity)

See the 3 concentric circles diagram; the embracing of Core beliefs, the presence of the Holy Spirit, and the influence of the objective truth are present in the spiritual heart.

With respect to a person's transformation, it begins in the heart and requires radical changes by embracing the objective truth. This author presents six scenarios and two personality disorder examples to demonstrate a constructive and realistic way of establishing a new way of life. One of the most basic ways that beliefs, from a Christian perspective, can shape reality is if you believe that you're capable, competent, and deserving of your dream job, you're probably more likely to notice and seek out opportunities that could help you get there. You're also more likely to perform well in an interview. Contrary to the common assumption that overconfidence can backfire, research suggests that it may actually be beneficial. Overconfident people tend to appear more socially skilled and higher in social status, even when those evaluating them have access to objective information about their actual ability.

Beliefs can also influence health behaviors. Research suggests that people are more likely to engage in health-promoting behaviors like eating well and exercising if they have a greater sense of self-efficacy—that is if they believe that they belong to God's family and live out principles and values in Holy Scripture.

Recall the seven scenarios presented in Section 3 of this book. With the help of this counselor, you, the reader, will see how the introduction to Objective Truth created a much different spirit and soul for the persons in the seven stories.

SCENARIO # 1: Regarding one of my clients, he shared that he leaves work and stops by the bar to get a drink of Vodka to calm him from his busy day at work and to gain the strength from the drink to face his demanding wife when he arrives home. This Client is showing his Reactions to ease the tension of events at work and to prepare for his trigger regarding his demanding wife.

So, addressing the three parts of the Soul with this Client:

First, the Client's mind is dominated by the brain's interpretation of the five senses in the Body. Second, the Client's emotional disposition of being mad from his thoughts (mind) of work and facing his wife triggers his reaction (body) to exhibit characteristics of passive-aggressive. Third, the combination of the thoughts in his mind and the emotions in his amygdala causes his desire (will) to consume the Vodka after work.

With the help of this counselor, Belief # ***9. Urge Self-control*** --- *Titus 2: 4 – 8* was introduced.

The husband realizes he has embraced the secular truth that drinking calms him from his work and eases his mind when facing his demanding wife. Thus, the husband now sees the beliefs behind all these reactions. It became apparent to the husband that his drinking works against himself and not for himself. His worldly truth in his spirit causes stinking thinking in his soul to affect: 1. Husband scares his wife with his drinking and driving, which causes an argument; 2. Husband is less sensitive to his wife and more selfish in his ways, and 3. He is teaching this truth to his children. This therapist drilled down with the husband in order to discover where this client obtained the truth and inspire the belief to consume the vodka drink.

His truth embraced comes from his perceptions and experiences (subjective truth) of life, such as his father did similar things. So he learned from his father.

Now, in order for transformation to occur, the husband needs to discover a new truth, an objective truth, to bring to life a new set of beliefs in his spirit. This therapist has encouraged the client to consider the objective truth that comes from our Creator. With the installment of this new objective truth, then the client is able to set a new course cluster of beliefs to impact the elements of the soul to respond – not react – to life's triggers.

SCENARIO #2 SQUEAKY WHEEL GETS THE GREASE --- Why does a person raise his voice with a harsh tone? He has learned from watching others that the squeaky wheel gets the grease. He feels like he's not being heard, so raising his voice will mean that others will hear him better and that his desires will be met. So, in his soul, he has developed these thoughts of the squeaky wheel getting the grease from his brain interpreting the five senses. So, as a result, he operates out of his soul.

With the help of this counselor, Belief # ***6. Plant TRUTH which can save from filth --- *** *James 1:21* inserted.

This person realizes he has embraced worldly truth, which develops from two sources: nurture and nature. Nature and nurture are theories that answer the question of how people become who they are. Nature describes the person's innate qualities, and nurture describes the personal experiences that help to determine a person's subjective beliefs, which direct their behaviors. This Therapist pointed to the Client to consider the Objective Truth of Scriptural principles that are not swayed by intellect or experiences. So, this Client established his protocol to understand God's wisdom. Understanding God is not the same as being book-smart or street-smart. By applying Scripture concepts, the squeaky wheel person gains a deeper understanding of how to think and live wisely rather than just human logic.

SCENARIO # 3 WORLDLY TRUTH IMPACTS FALSE BELIEFS ---- The Client has said that he had no part in the demise of his three previous marriages. He did nothing wrong in any of them and doesn't carry any baggage from the previous marriages into his current relationship.

FALSE BELIEF: There are some people who believe that their past relationships do not impact their current relationship situation. Unbeknownst to this gentleman, he has conveyed a **belief.** If this person has truly not made peace with his past and put the past where it belongs - in the past, then this person's belief can cause some stinky thinking and cause him to react to life's events presently. Please see how beliefs (in the Spirit) are deeper than thoughts (in the Soul) and how they can affect embracing worldwide Truth. This Subjective Truth influences how a person makes decisions, which results in passive or aggressive reactions.

With the guidance of this counselor, Belief # ***3. Transforms the Mind --*** *Romans 12:2* was engaged.

This client was directed to consider worldly truth versus God's truth. As the client was challenged by the true qualities of a leader, all parties involved would validate the proper execution of Colossians 3: 12 -13, which describes the leadership qualities of kindness, compassion, humility, gentleness, and forgiveness.

Dear Reader, are you living with false beliefs of worldly truth or the authentic qualities of Scriptural truth?

SCENARIO # 4 EMPHASIS ON BELIEFS: When a person experiences trauma, he may develop beliefs that the world is unsafe and unpredictable. Most authors do not continue to emphasize the importance of the concept of beliefs. This author wants to strictly, specifically, and with great detail emphasize the issue of beliefs. Many of us simply convey what appears as our thoughts, but when we are challenged, encouraged, or when we make an effort to look much deeper into these thoughts, they convey beliefs that we then operate.

BELIEF: For example, Why did the Client commit Infidelity? .... to send a firm message to his wife? ....

1. ALCOHOL --- The Client consumed alcohol, which became a trigger to open the door to inappropriate behaviors (body) like infidelity to communicate a message to his

spouse. What is this Client's Belief that converts into a thought?

2. The client and co-workers were at a Training out of town at a Hotel. The female co-worker asked the Client to stay in her hotel room for the evening to talk. She said the Client was easy to talk to --- she was learning skills for a new job and wanted to talk about her day. She was drunk. She started kissing the Client. The Client felt a moment of relief. He shared that this encounter felt nice ---- all the problems were gone ... exploring a new adventure. At that time, the Client was not sure what he wanted. Because this event occurred with a co-worker, then the Client was unsure about staying married to his wife.

3. The client had previous experience with this female co-worker at work. He kissed her on three different occasions and was not caught or confronted by anyone. He saw he could get away with it. He felt too comfortable with her for the last incident. She asked the Client to stay because he was easy to talk with. Then, because they were out of town and out of the office at a hotel, no one would find out about his encounter with this female co-worker. The client encountered sex with her since he got away with these intimate moments the 3 times before. This Therapist presented the 3 concentric circles

(see diagram) and showed him how his belief in getting away with the encounters with the female co-worker shaped his thoughts and feelings on this last encounter and caused his will to set his behaviors to go further with sexual intimate encounters with this girl. So, this is why the Client committed the Infidelity and now is troubled by the guilt, shame, and pain of hurting his wife.

With the help of this Counselor, Belief # ***15. Show Respect* --- *1 Peter 2: 16, 17*** needed to be engaged.

Verse 16 says: "Live as free people, but do not use your freedom as a coverup for evil." This Therapist took the opportunity to show how his BELIEF was formed because he had not experienced consequences with the other 3 times before. No person is capable of making this transformation on their own strength, so each person must be empowered with Belief # ***8. Empowered with extra-ordinary strength* ---- *Philippians 4:13***

As a licensed Therapist, I work with all sorts of individuals diagnosed with Mood and Personality Disorders. One group of folks I assist is those diagnosed with Narcissism. Beliefs of a Narcissist are the root cause of this disorder.

SCENARIO # 5 ***Narcissistic Personality Disorder*** (NPD) is one of 10 personality disorders presented in the fifth edition of the *Diagnostic and Statistical Manual of Mental Disorders* (DSM-5), the Industry standards we counselors are required to follow. The dominant signs of NPD include an inflated sense of self-importance, a lack of empathy for others, and a deep need for constant attention or admiration. Their BELIEF SYSTEM manifests grandiose fantasies about themselves (i.e., *they're smarter, more attractive, and more successful than everyone they know*), easily put other people down, and generally hijack any conversation or situation to make themselves feel better or superior. A narcissist is very uncomfortable feeling "less than perfect," and they'll protect themselves at all costs. For a Narcissist, it starts with what they **BELIEVE**!

With the help of this counselor, Belief # ***4. Sheds light on one's inmost being --*** *Proverbs 20:27, 29* was engaged.

The Narcissistic client, in order to make the transformation, should grasp what Proverbs 16 says, "It is much better for you to be wise and sensible than to be rich....Too much pride will destroy you. You are better off to be humble and poor than to get rich from what you take by force." "Good sense is a fountain that gives life, but fools are punished by their reactive foolishness." (Proverbs 16:22). According to 2 Timothy, this verse says that in the last days, people will love themselves, which is a characteristic of reactive narcissistic behavior **Constructive Side:** A narcissistic client embracing grandiose views of themselves are mentally tougher, less stressed, and less at risk for depression. This Therapist encourages the narcissist to follow Objective Truth to excel in this mental strength.

For those who live with a Narcissist, the Bible reminds them to set boundaries: "Above all else, guard your heart, for everything you do flows from it." (Proverbs 4:23). Each partner should not fight a Narcissist's fire with fire. Luke 6 says, "…do good to those who hate you, bless those who curse you, pray for those who mistreat you." (v27-28)

SCENARIO # 6 As I was working with one of my clients recently, she expressed concern that her husband has changed. From her perspective, she indicates that he seems to not have as much interest in her now, married almost 30 years. She has come to therapy to work on herself. She conveys to this Therapist that she feels she's no longer pretty because of her gray hair and the change in her body contour. She states that she is insecure about herself and her looks, thus stating her beliefs based upon what truth? Is the Truth based on her husband's preference?

This therapist takes the opportunity to present the three concentric circles in order to bring about a change. This therapist helped the client understand that her thoughts and feelings, which bring about insecurity, are her beliefs. She believes she is not attractive. See the concentric diagram. As you can see from the diagram, many people believe that to bring about change, you must start working from the outside (change of behaviors) to the inward (eventually, change of beliefs). In other words, changing our reactions, which most people hope to change thoughts, will transform the spirit inside of us. However, transformation occurs from starting with Objective TRUTH, which impacts beliefs on the inside and empowers working on a person's outward presentation, which means we change the way we believe about ourselves, our relationships, or how we view the world. When we change the way we believe and rid ourselves of false beliefs, then we let go of the stinking thinking and take on more appropriate healthy thoughts, which makes us take control of our emotions and feelings so that our will to direct our behaviors becomes a much more Healthier way to approach life, to take responsibility for our souls, and to respond rather than react to life's circumstances.

The client did not realize that her thoughts were actually her beliefs. She said no one has ever shown her that in the past. This therapist showed her that our beliefs become the truth for which we live. Is that correct? So you must ask yourself that question: what truth am I building my beliefs upon? With respect to this client, the truth became evident that her beauty was her loyalty to her husband, her sensitivity, and the external issue that her husband, over the years, has declined in his mental strength.

So, the question is to ask yourself, what truth are you building your beliefs upon?

With the help of this Counselor, Belief # ***10. Presents Integrity ---*** *Psalm 41:12* was introduced.

The client began to see that her beliefs direct her thoughts, which impact her behaviors. This therapist showed the client that she must change the way she believes about her beauty. When she began to accept the belief that beauty is more than just the external, her belief in herself became stronger. This new belief about herself resulted in greater confidence in her cognition, evoked much healthier feelings about herself, and responded not to react to her husband's perspective.

SCENARIO #7: EXAMPLE: Counseling sessions with Dave (the name is changed to comply with HIPPA)

He was troubled because his wife's illness was serious, and if his wife died, then he would need to care for her four children, and his family did not want Dave to neglect his biological daughter. He is concerned about his BELIEF, which is that one day, the kids may not see him as their father. The neglect of his daughter will make him angry that he tried to be a father to his biological and stepchildren together.

This discussion caused this Therapist to bring out the 3 CONCENTRIC CIRCLES. His BELIEF of stepchildren in the future may cause him to act and make decisions today in a certain way. Today, these stepchildren see Dave as their dad.

This Client shares about his biological dad, who took responsibility for his stepsisters. This Therapist challenged the Client to ask his bio father if years ago his father questioned his role to be a father to children and stepchildren and from what he BELIEVED that he did or did not ponder to be a father to all the kids. The father accepted his role, which demonstrated a BELIEF.

With the help of this Counselor, Belief #***20 – Responsibility – Galatians 6 & #21 – Kindness - Galatians 5:22***

This Therapist brought to the Client's attention that the reason the Client was presented with this situation is that GOD presents the situation now of his role as father to children and stepchildren because Dave was prepared to tackle his current situation by what he experienced (similar situation) as the biological child with his father. This Therapist asked the Client if he felt he was neglected by his father because his father cared for you and your stepsisters. The Client replied no. Then this Therapist asked if the stepsisters think less of his father because they were cared for by their stepfather. Ct replied NO.

This Therapist brought to light the 3 CONCENTRIC circles that his deep BELIEFS of insecurity of the current situation or the future are impacting his thoughts, feelings, and his will to React or Respond. But God has put Dave with Sabrina so he can be the father of her children (stepchildren) like his father was to his step sisters. It is amazing how God prepares us for future experiences, such as what the client is dealing with today, in light of his experience as a child. So, this Therapist encouraged the Client to address his belief of insecurity to see the purpose and not surrender to his insecurity but to Respond in an assertive way to care for all the children if his wife passes from this life.

Next, this author presents two personality disorder examples to explore in a constructive and realistic way for establishing a new way of life

ANTISOCIAL PERSONALITY DISORDER:

The Bottom Line

An Antisocial Personality Disordered person is one who does not care what is right or wrong, has no regard for consequences, does not learn from experience, is indifferent to what happens to other people, and is willing to do anything in order to get what they want, and will harm anyone who interferes with them.

SO NOW IT REQUIRES TRANSFORMATION to introduce the Gospel of Truth to this person with this Disorder. This person allows the presence of the Holy Spirit, presented on page 75. With a manifestation of 21 qualities, see page 76.

BORDERLINE PERSONALITY DISORDER:

The Bottom Line

A Borderline Personality Disorder person is one who is erratic, unpredictable, overly intense, shifts between extreme states of mood/thinking/love / and hate, and lacks a clear sense of self or concept of "who" they are.

SO NOW IT REQUIRES TRANSFORMATION to introduce the Gospel of Truth to this person with this Disorder. This person allows the presence of the Holy Spirit, presented on page 40, with the manifestation of 21 qualities. See page 41.

Exploring these scenarios and examples should have empowered the reader to see there's more to life than just The brain and the five senses.

HOW CAN YOU HARNESS THE POWER OF BELIEF TO IMPROVE YOUR LIFE?

For one, you can engage in practices that change **your habitual way** of thinking, such as keeping a gratitude journal or learning mindfulness meditation. These practices can help you notice and appreciate the good in life and keep you from getting caught up in unconstructive, negative thoughts.

Second, you can **set clear intentions** for how you want to approach each day and make an effort to align your behavior with the TRUTH. When things don't go your way, you'll know that you're moving in the right direction.

THIRD, a strong **faith** in God's principles can help to cope with the stress experienced in life and enable the impact of that stress to be less significant. Without a strong personal faith in the values of God, we must resort to our own resources to cope with the stress present in our lives. Often, we attempt to cope with this stress through addictions and other methods of escape, like verbally abusive displays. This behavior can further exacerbate the effect of stress on our physical health. A strong personal faith in Christ Jesus can be a resource that helps to manage stress.

Our beliefs and attitudes, determined to a large degree by our faith, will play a major role in our thinking patterns. Our day-to-day thinking will have an impact on our emotions and feelings, and our emotions and feelings will have a major impact on our behaviors. In this regard, our thought patterns play a significant role in our emotional and physical health.

And finally, you can recognize that while beliefs may be powerful, they are certainly not all-powerful, and life is full of suffering that we neither invite nor deserve.

God has given the reader the Holy Spirit by faith, which imparts unconditional love (Romans 5:5) in the spirit of His children. His Truth lets' all persons know that because of Christ's suffering, believers will be given what God has promised (Romans 8:16-18). The person who incorporates the Scriptural Truth is empowered to overcome a secular mindset and embrace extraordinary strength from God's Spirit that lives in a person's spirit (Romans 8:9-10).

***TRANSITION from Spirit to Soul: SUBCONSCIOUSNESS - Faith* (Romans 5:2, Galatians 5:5)**

Subconsciousness is the bridge between spirit and soul that notices and remembers information when you're not actively trying to do so, and it influences your thoughts or behavior even though you don't fully realize it.

1st THESSALONIANS 5:23 (FBV) – "May the God of peace himself make you completely holy, and may your whole being -- body, soul, and spirit -- be kept blameless for when our Lord Jesus Christ returns."

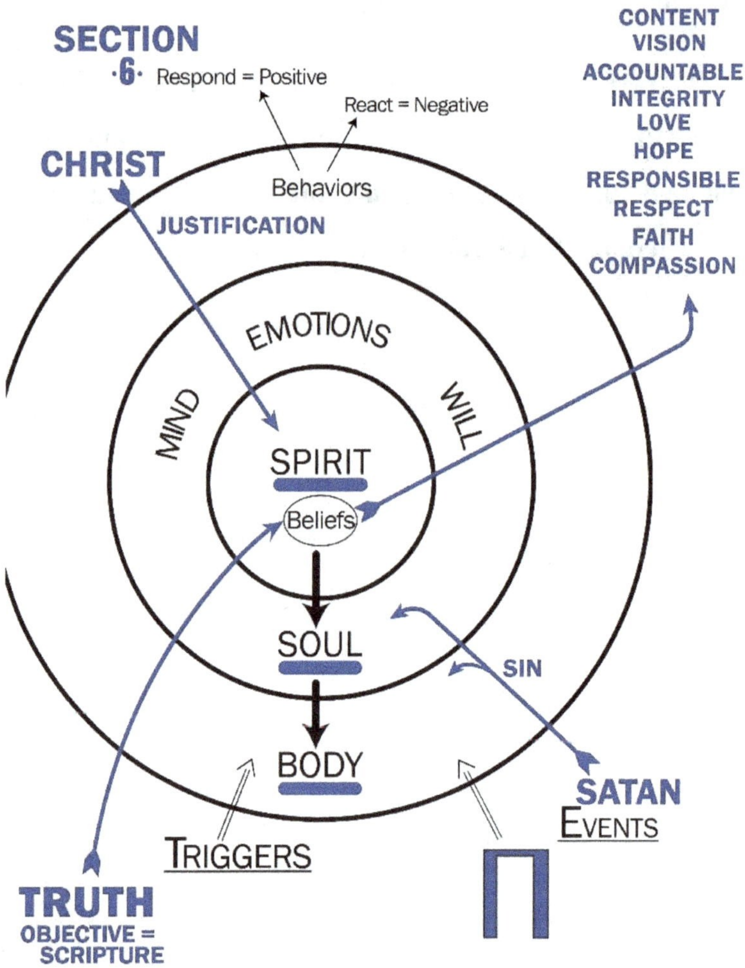
SECTION
·6·
Respond = Positive
React = Negative
CHRIST
Behaviors
JUSTIFICATION
CONTENT
VISION
ACCOUNTABLE
INTEGRITY
LOVE
HOPE
RESPONSIBLE
RESPECT
FAITH
COMPASSION
EMOTIONS
MIND
WILL
SPIRIT
Beliefs
SOUL
SIN
BODY
SATAN
EVENTS
TRIGGERS
TRUTH
OBJECTIVE =
SCRIPTURE

SECTION # 6

14. SOUL ---

The SOUL is the second Concentric Circle and the connector between the Spirit and the Body. It translates and transfers the essence of the Spirit into the behaviors of the Body.

Remember Section 2: Our soul's purpose is why we are here on this earth at this time. What we are looking for or seeking is probably connected to our soul's purpose.

The Soul can be transformed now by surrendering to the outside TRUTH from the Creator of the Universe and thus renewing the mind, changing attitude, aligning feelings to cognition, conforming values to the truth and uniting the WILL not to perceptions of reality but to the TRUTH that is deeper and more universal than perceptions or personal thoughts.

When the Soul agrees with the Spirit by aligning with the TRUTH, double-mindedness does not occur.

What is TRUTH? Recall the concepts presented in Section 4.

Is Truth your perception? Is Truth based upon societal rules, rituals, or popular thinking? On the contrary…

TRUTH

TRUTH IS THE BASIS AND FOUNDATION OF HOW PEOPLE SHOULD ACT, HOW PEOPLE SHOULD MAKE DECISIONS, AND HAVE HEALTHY RELATIONS WITH OTHERS. Truth in our life provides guidance, wisdom, strength, courage, motivation, comfort, faith, and purpose. TRUTH IS THE WISDOM OF GOD.

The TRUTH of the Gospel introduced will manifest peace (not happiness), constructive power, patience, and perseverance, which lead to victory, joy, prosperity, endurance, and the ability to respond to life in healthy ways. The introduction of humbling oneself to the Gospel -- - becoming a part of the family of God -- is the only quality instituted to strengthen a person's mental health and conquer mental illness in a person's Soul.

Scripture passages to declare the TRUTH of God's design for his children.

James 1: (Believers) consider it pure joy whenever you face trials of many kinds because the testing of your faith produces perseverance. Let perseverance finish its work so that you may be mature and not lack wisdom. Blessed is the one who perseveres under trial; that person will receive the crown of life that the Lord has promised to those who love Him.

1 Timothy 6: Godliness with contentment is great gain. Believers pursue righteousness, godliness, faith, love, endurance, and gentleness. Command the rich person not to put his hope in wealth but to put his hope in God, who richly provides believers with everything for enjoyment.

Proverbs 21: whoever pursues righteousness and love finds life, prosperity, and honor. (Couples) Those who guard their mouths and their tongues keep themselves from calamity. The horse (what is your horse?) is made ready for the day of battle, but victory rests with the Lord.

James 3 (AMPC): *PEACE = peacemaker, not peacekeeper*: The <u>wisdom from God</u> is first of all pure, then it is peace-loving, courteous. It is willing to yield to reason, full of compassion and good fruits. It is wholehearted and straightforward., free from doubts, wavering, and insecurity. Righteousness is sown in peace by those who work for and make peace in themselves and in others. Peace means concord, agreement, and harmony between individuals and couples with undisturbedness in a peaceful mind free from fears, agitating passions, and moral conflicts.

RECALL EARLIER IN THE BOOK ABOUT THE **HISTORY** OF THE DESCRIPTION OF THE SOUL

THOMAS AQUINAS

According to Thomas Aquinas, the soul is conditioned by the body, just as the body is conditioned by the soul. However, Thomas Aquinas's philosophy falls short of the concepts of the Soul and Body. **This author/ counselor presents the fact that the body is dependent upon the soul. Thus, mutual conditioning is wrong in that the soul is also dependent upon the body.** If the soul really assumes the body into its own existence, as Thomas Aquinas maintains, the body cannot be considered alien to the soul. It is the soul's body and nothing else.

This author presents from a Godly, Christian viewpoint the strength, logistics, and benefits of mental health, which enables a person to cope with the stresses of life, realize their abilities, contribute to their community, and display strong social interactive well-being demonstrating the Soul's directive upon the Body.

PLATO

Logistikon, as described by Plato, is the part of the soul that loves logic, thought, and rational learning aimed at truth, which manifests mental health. A person who accepts and lives out the TRUTH from the Creator, God is empowered with these characteristics of logic, reasoning, rational quality, and knowledge.

This author wants to bring the wisdom from these historical, philosophical leaders to our contemporary culture. These attributes and characteristics presented in history did not become permanent mental and physical healthcare concepts. This author is going to show all readers the benefits of understanding the functions of these attributes and characteristics to transform lives that historic philosophy leaders presented (Remember from Section #2: Our soul acts as a valve between the spirit and the body).

Soul contains 3 Parts:

Soul= Thoughts (Mind)+ Feelings (Amygdala) + Free will (Temporal) (see 3 Concentric Circles): MIND, EMOTIONS, AND FREE WILL, which should empower every person to see that they are created humans (not as ROBOTS) with the components to freely choose to honor, respect, and follow the Creator of the Universe.

SOUL = 1. MIND

***Remember Section 2*: THE SECULAR MIND IS DOMINATED BY WHAT A PERSON CAN *SEE, TASTE, HEAR, SMELL,* and *FEEL,* or what *BRAIN* interprets. There is more to life than these elements --- so let's explore.**

Frontal Lobes

The largest lobes of the cerebral cortex are the frontal lobes. These are located at the front of the brain behind the forehead. The BRAIN controls a person's movements and various bodily functions; the MIND contributes to a person's morality, reasoning, and understanding.

The MIND is the frontal lobe of the Brain. The frontal lobe's functions primarily involve 'higher' cognitive functions such as decision-making, conscious thought, problem-solving, and attention.

Mind (Stinking or Healthy Thinking, naturally free, controls morality, reasoning and understanding, knowledge)

The Mind: This is clearly and definitely proved by the Word of God. Proverbs 2:10 gives us the spiritual ground to prove that the mind is a part of the soul. This verse says, "Wisdom will enter your heart, and knowledge will be pleasant to your soul." Because knowledge is a matter of the mind, this proves that the mind is a part of the soul. Proverbs 19:21 and 24:14 also indicate that knowledge and wisdom are related to the soul. In addition, Psalm 139:14 says, "My soul knows it well." Since to know is a matter of the mind, this also proves that the mind must be a part of the soul. Psalm 13:2 speaks of bearing concern in the soul. This concern must be considered. Lamentations 3:20 says, "My soul remembers them well," indicating that the soul can remember things. Through these verses, we can be clear that the mind is the organ that knows, considers, and remembers and is a part of the soul.

Transformation by renewing of the mind - Romans 12:2, Holy Bible.

The verses of the Scriptures above are grounds for saying that within the soul, there are three parts—the mind as the leading part with the will and the emotion. These are the best verses to prove this, but they are not the only ones. If we study the entire Scriptures, it is hard to find anything other than these three parts in the soul. These three parts comprise all the functions of the soul.

Double-Minded

When our Soul (thoughts) does not agree with the Spirit (Beliefs), double-mindedness occurs, so James 4:8 says,

"Purify your hearts, you double-minded." The Scripture continues to say, "Come near to God, and he will come near to you." A double-minded man is unstable in all his ways (James 1:5-8). If anyone lacks wisdom, that person should ask God, who gives generously to all. But when a person asks, that person must believe and not doubt – such a person is double-minded and unstable in all he does.

Dear Reader, let's explore some examples to help you better understand

A. Why can't you be happy? The focus should be on Content, not Happiness.

CONTENT is more solid and stable compared to the diligent pursuit of being *Happy.*

The first thing to realize is **happiness** has to do with a happening like a party or a celebration. But what is life like when there are no constant happenings? What are the skills and tools that help you be OK when those things are not happening? The Holy Scriptures emphasize the call to pursue contentment.

B. Have you ever tried to push away a negative thought only to feel it grow stronger? There's a saying — "What you resist, persists," — and when it comes to our mindset, this couldn't be more true.

Instead of ignoring those thoughts as Peace-Keeping, incorporate the Truth of **PEACE-MAKING,** which sets up the power to acknowledge and reframe those thoughts into something that fuels your growth.

This powerful technique, called Cognitive Reframing, helps shift mindsets, whether facing partner relations, business challenges, or personal setbacks.

C. Remember the presentation of Sexuality determination in Section 2.

The overabundance of testosterone in females and the lack of testosterone in males can suggest that a person is a different sex type than the body the person lives in.

Joe Herbert M.B, Ph.D.

Hormones and the Brain

Summary: So too much testosterone or estrogen in the body activates the brain (androgen receptor) to live life according to the five senses of the body: see, taste, hear, smell, and feel, which results in a REACT to facing life's triggers [see the Diagram] which becomes described as the Secular Mind.

These groups are unhealthy and need the injection of the Truth of the Gospel to be transformed in their Soul (see the Section

6 diagram). So, many people would conclude that testosterone impacts the Brain, which is dominated by the five senses to determine a person's sexuality. But when a person employs medication or medical assistance with the testosterone or estrogen and embraces the TRUTH, the objective Truth, the mind becomes empowered to consciously apply the wise understanding of sexuality instead of the brain conforming to the chemical imbalance in the body and listening to the five senses.

D. MENTAL HEALTH trends:

VICTIM – a person who allows toxic thoughts, blame, and shame toward others or feeling harmed.

Instead, the Objective Truth of the Creator is to manifest the character of VICTOR as a person who brings thoughts into obedience to Righteousness.

Constructive mental health happens when a person realizes they need to respond, not react to life's triggers. A person who incorporates foundational truths of Objective Truth in order to eradicate stinking thinking (mind) then moves to the following components:

- **meaning and purpose**: feeling your life is valuable and worthwhile

- **resilience**: the ability to cope with the stresses of daily life
- **optimism**: feeling positive about your life and future
- **self-esteem**: feeling positive about yourself
- having **positive relationships**: people you care for and who care for you
- a **sense of accomplishment**: doing things that give you a sense of achievement or competence
- **emotional stability**: feeling calm and able to manage emotions
- experiencing **positive emotions**: content, fun, joy, pride, satisfaction, and love
- **vitality**: feeling energetic.

So, a person who realizes the necessity for the above components to manifest healthy mental health and mental well-being will find it extremely difficult to conjure up or manifest these qualities. The person must be willing to open up their philosophy of life to a new way of life to see drastic change occur, gain the strength and power of the mind, and manifest mental well-being. This new philosophy lets go of the victim state and embodies the character of **VICTOR.** The victor takes responsibility to find a solution, is not afraid to face problems, never makes excuses, works towards goals, is proactive, demonstrates resilience, works to make peace with others, exhibits forgiveness, and many more.

Psalms 149:4-5 "For the Lord takes delight in his people; he crowns the humble with victory. Let his faithful people rejoice in this honor."

E. SERIOUS VIOLATIONS: We need to ask ourselves if we are committing one of these serious mental sins.

Lust – 1 Thessalonians 4:4-6

Gluttony -- Philippian 3:18-19

Greed --- Romans 1:29 - 32

Sloth --- Proverbs 10:4

Wrath -- Ephesians 4

Envy – Mark 7:21- 23

Pride – 1 Peter 5:5 -6~~, 1 John 5:4~~

A believer with God's spirit empowers the transformation of the Mind from stinking thinking to reasonable thinking, conforms values from perceived truth to objective truth, pursues contentment versus happiness, is empowered to freely choose to honor the Creator, develop perseverance to become mature and not lack wisdom, free of doubts, eradicate toxic thoughts. Faith in the Son of God is what gives each believer this victory to overcome the insanity of the world. (1 John 5: 4).

MORE SERIOUS VIOLATIONS

Romans 12:2 (a person is renewed by the transformation of the MIND), not the BRAIN.

The Mind renewed overcomes these public disgraces:

BLAME

SHAME

GUILT

NARCISSIST

PEOPLE PLEASER

INADEQUATE

INSECURITY

OBSESSIVE-COMPULSIVE DISORDER

The reasoning of the mind goes to a Limit ---- so FAITH in the Higher Power enters to bring extraordinary strength to overpower these negative and destructive qualities. However, a spiritual element most of the time invades to distract or circumvent a person attempting to move in a constructive trajectory.

PRESENCE OF SPIRITUAL DECEPTION – SATAN – manifested as SIN – influencing the Soul & Body

A broken relationship with the creator opens the door to spiritual deception that influences the Body and Soul as described:

1. COMMISSION --- a person exchanges truth for a lie -- Romans 1:19 -32
2. OMISSION ---- Something neglected, left out, or left undone -- James 4:17
3. DISPOSITION ---- Hurt people hurt people -- Proverbs 16:27; people will embrace false beliefs -- 2 Peter 2:2

Don't let Satan trigger you with the thoughts he presents in your head: Deceive, Entice, Failure, Negativity, Condemn, Selfishness.

Shortly before my alarm sounds each morning, my mind starts overthinking. As I reflect back, I am not making a conscious effort to think about the past. My mind recalls all of the bad things I've done. If I am waking up to a new day, why does my mind bring up the evilness of my past and not the good things I've done or the pleasures that I have experienced? That, my friends, is the spiritual Deception of this world. So, to convert, I have to bring every thought captive to the obedience of Christ, 2 Corinthians 10, verse five. I am transformed by the renewing of my mind. (Romans 12:2).

F. Mindfulness: By incorporating Objective Truth, the concept of Mindfulness can help a person focus on the present, embrace their purpose, be more content over happiness, and be positive when faced with obstacles and challenges. Also, it can help a person understand themselves better and exhibit better listening qualities.

The cerebral cortex, the mind, which is the outer surface of the brain, serves many conscious and unconscious functions, such as being responsible for movement, processing sensory information from the senses, processing language, intelligence, and personality. Knowledge of the function of the Cortex should empower every person to the wonderful, deliberate, and intentional involvement of a Higher Power.

Recall the concepts of truth affecting the mind as we move to connect Emotions affected by the truth as best described in the Holy Scripture: **2 Timothy 1:7**: God did not give us a spirit of fear, but the spirit of power, unconditional love, and self-discipline.

SOUL = 2. EMOTIONS ***(from Amygdala): see Feeling Wheel – only four emotions!***

Romans 12:17 -- mad

Matthew 5:4 --- sad

1 Thessalonians 5:16-18 --- glad

2 Timothy 1:7 --- afraid

Many times, when a person allows their emotions to dominate, the Amygdala ***releases hormones into the body, which may encourage a person to react to*** their behavior. So Objective Truth presents the person with putting their mind in gear before engaging their emotions. This proves that within the soul, this is the organ and function of the emotion.

EMOTIONS conveyed in a new philosophy of life:

The emotion comprises many things, including love, hatred, joy, and grief. Song of Songs 1:7 and Psalm 42:1 show us that to love is a function of the soul. This proves that within the soul, there is the organ, the function, and the emotion. Second, Samuel 5:8, Psalm 107:18, and Ezekiel 36:5 show us that hating, loathing, and despising are also in the soul. Despising in the soul is the hatred of the soul. Since these are emotions, this also proves that the emotion must be a part of the soul.

Joy is a great part of the emotion. Isaiah 61:10 and Psalm 86:4 tell us that joy is in the soul. This again proves that the emotion is a part of the soul. Deuteronomy 14:26 and Jeremiah 22:27 tell us that the soul desires. According to the better translations and Strong's or Young's concordances, *desire* in Jeremiah 44:14 and *set their heart* in Ezekiel 24:25 literally *lift up the soul.* These verses tell us that the desire for emotion is something in our soul. In addition, 1 Samuel 30:6, Judges 10:16, and Job 30:25 speak of bitterness, misery, and grief in the soul.

Healing happens when a traumatized person re-evaluates thoughts and emotions and recalls awareness of the objective TRUTH to refresh beliefs (in Spirit) and thoughts (in Soul) to respond, not react.

<u>Dear Reader, let's explore some examples to help you better understand</u>

A. Happy -

Everyone wants to be happy. Happiness is the feeling, the outcome, and the by product. The focus should be the pursuit of holiness and a deeper state of well-being. Happiness occurs with celebrations, parties, and "happenings." If you don't have parties going on constantly. Then what? Our goal must be to achieve CONTENT, not happiness. "Delight yourself in the

Lord, and he will give you the desires of your heart." (Psalm 37:4)

B. Guilt

There are three basic kinds of guilt: (1) **natural guilt**, or remorse over something you did or failed to do; (example) Yes, I confess that I gave away God's money that he offered/provided to me to become self-employed. Believe me! I beat myself up every day - trying to forgive myself every day! (2) **free-floating, or toxic guilt**—the underlying sense of not being a good person; and (3) **existential guilt**, the negative feeling that arises out of the injustice you perceive in the world and out of your own unpaid obligations to life itself.

The emotion of Guilt can project into two different directions:

GUILT - good guilt - brings CONVICTION --- Leads to the need to repent and be TRANSFORMED

GUILT – bad guilt – brings CONDEMNATION --- Leads to hopelessness and DESPAIR

Not only are these concepts true for Guilt, but they are also accurate for the following: **Shame, Fear, and Blame.** Replace Guilt with each of these three words, and it will manifest in the remainder of the sentence.

(EMOTIONS) So deaden the power of the evil desires lurking in your body, such as Sexual immorality, moral corruption, lust, evil desire, and greed. Also, set aside anger, rage, malice, slander, obscene language, and lies. Put on the new nature which is renewed in knowledge. Choose the emotions of compassion, kindness, humility, gentleness, patience, tolerance, peace, thankfulness, and forgiveness. And over all, these virtues put on love, which binds them all together in perfect unity. (Colossians 3:5-14 CEB)

Soul = 3. + Free WILL: *(Endocrine System, Immune System and the Nerve System)*

Job 7:15 says, "My soul would choose," and 6:7 says, "My soul refuses." To choose and to refuse are both decisions and functions of the will. These passages prove that the will must be a part of the soul. First Chronicles 22:19 says, "Now set your heart and your soul to seek after Jehovah your God." Just as we set our mind to think, this verse says that we set our soul to seek. This is, of course, to make a decision. That the soul makes a decision also proves that the will is a part of the soul. Numbers 30:2 says, "When a man vows a vow to Jehovah or swears an oath to bind himself by pledge..."

The term *to bind oneself,* which occurs eleven times in this chapter, literally means "to bind one's soul." **To bind the soul is to make a decision**. This chapter in numbers deals with vows made to the Lord. Since we must make a decision to bind our soul to vow to the Lord, this also proves that the will must be a part of the soul. It would be good for the brothers and sisters, especially the young ones, to remember all these verses. They should pick up the burden of learning this. *Philippians 4 -- desire, choice, intention to act*

(WILL) God's word is alive and powerful. It is sharper than any double-edged sword. His word can cut through our spirit and soul, through our joints and marrow, until it discovers the desires and thoughts of our soul. (Hebrews 4:12) As a result, they don't live the rest of their human lives determined by human desires but in ways determined by God's will. (Peter 4:2 CEB). When a person chose freely to be compelled to sin, what consequences did that person receive for doing things that now ashamed of? (Romans 6) His friends might say to him: How is that working for you? But now, being made free from sin and becoming servants to God by your own free will, you have your fruit in holiness. (Romans 6: 22 KJV)

This therapist/author encourages each person to consider **GOALS and OBJECTIVES** presented to encourage the transformation of the Soul:

1. Achieve to discover a new mental framework for addressing difficult situations, overwhelmed emotional feelings, stinking thinking, and challenging relationships.

2. Recognize triggers to anger, types of anger, coping skills to manage anger, fear, triggers to fear, or self-destructive ways. Do not allow triggers to cause REACTIONS, but learn how to RESPOND to triggers.

3. Develop skills to relate with adults and peers in healthy relationships and not adversarial relationships by means of communication, expressing needs,. willingness to receive wisdom, accept positive influence

4. Admits personal responsibility for life chores, mistakes, personal or professional decisions, and addressing issues without the need for fight or flight. So the SOUL fashioned in the image of GOD evokes MINDFULNESS, which brings these BENEFITS-

1. Experience and express forgiveness
2. Activate TRUST
3. ACCEPT the difference between Mature and Perfectionism
4. Be transparent
5. Open to Criticism
6. Able to relax around others.
7. Realize God disciplines me out of LOVE rather than punish me out of ANGER.
8. EXPERIENCE patience and kindness with self & others
9. Exhibit Self Confidence
10. Demonstrate Courage
11. Live peaceably with People.

When we come to God in worship, we express our thanksgiving with our souls through songs of praise to Him for who He is and for what He has done in our lives; as Mary said, "My soul glorifies the Lord, and my spirit rejoices in God my Savior" (Luke 1:46-47, NIV). SOUL IS THE CONNECTOR BETWEEN THE BODY AND THE SPIRIT –

- **resilience**
- **optimism**
- **self-esteem**
- **meaning and purpose**
- having **positive relationships**
- a **sense of accomplishment**
- **emotional stability**
- experiencing **positive emotions**
- **vitality**: feeling energetic.

***Transition from Soul to Body: CONSCIOUSNESS --- *****Attitude (2 Corinthians 1:12) (Proverbs 20:9)**

Attitudes are thought to have three components: an affective component (feelings), a behavioral component (the effect of the attitude on behavior), and a cognitive component (belief and knowledge). Attitude is a position of the body properly derived from the Soul's 3 parts.

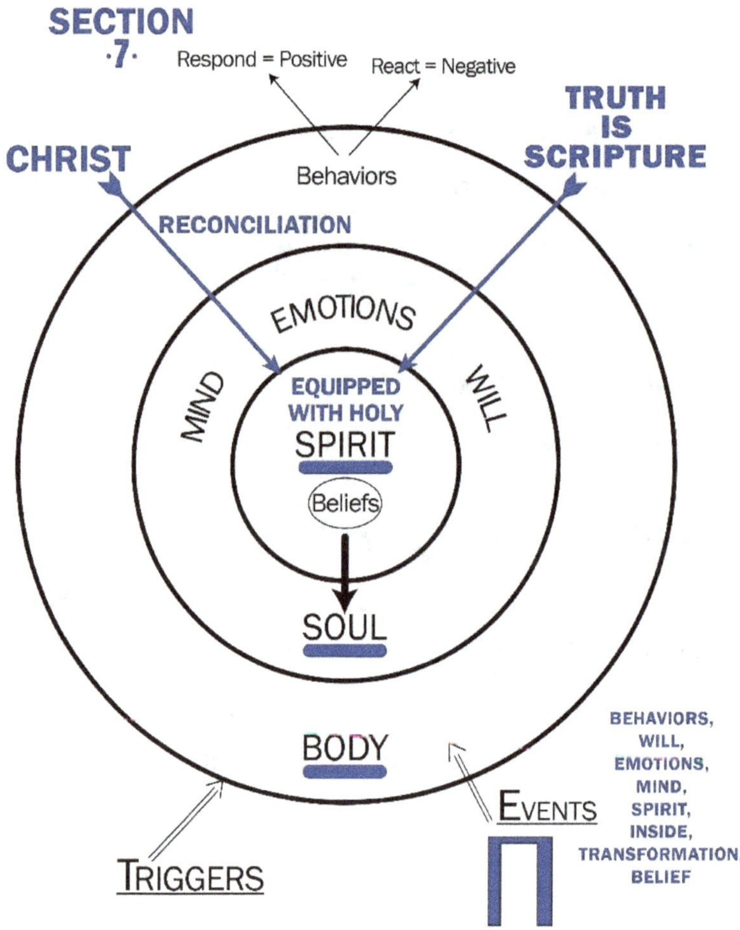
SECTION
·7·
Respond = Positive
React = Negative
TRUTH
IS
SCRIPTURE
CHRIST
Behaviors
RECONCILIATION
EMOTIONS
MIND
WILL
EQUIPPED
WITH HOLY
SPIRIT
Beliefs
SOUL
BODY
BEHAVIORS,
WILL,
EMOTIONS,
MIND,
SPIRIT,
INSIDE,
TRANSFORMATION,
BELIEF
EVENTS
TRIGGERS

SECTION # 7

BODY - FLESH (The Brain in the body interprets perceptions of the ears, hands, eyes, or the five senses – sight, smell, hear, taste, touch) **"The mind governed by the flesh (Body) is demise, but the mind governed by the Spirit is life and peace." (Romans 8:6)**

When the SOUL agrees with the SPIRIT by the injection of Objective TRUTH, the abundant life that God has designed will manifest itself in the BODY.

THE PRESENCE OF A PERSON'S BODY IS CONSTANTLY FACED WITH EXTERNAL TRIGGERS:

EVENTS, DILEMMAS, DIFFERENCES, HYPOCRISY, CONFUSION, DISTRESS, FLAGRANT, OBSTACLES, CHALLENGES, TEMPTATIONS, STRESS, CRAZINESS, NAKEDNESS, FLIRTING, CRITICAL, VERBAL ATTACK

THESE TRIGGERS IMPACT THE COMPONENTS OF THE BODY

BODY --- CHEMICAL IMBALANCES

Anxiety, ADD, ADHD, ASTHMA, Diabetes, High blood pressure, Hypertension, NEUROTRANSMITTERS like Serotonins & Dopamines, high Testosterone level, Estrogen level, Lymph nodes, Peptic Ulcer, Schizophrenia, Hormone imbalance. Recall earlier in the book; this author challenged the reader to consider the chemical imbalance of the BODY to cause **Gender determination** and imbalance of the BODY to empower **sex addicts** (Section 2). These Chemical Imbalances faced with life's triggers and circumstances cause each person to have to take on the responsibility to dig deep inside and remind themselves what they believe, which influences the way they think, feel, and act. So, with Objective Truth, it becomes imperative that a person realize the impact of imbalance in their body on healthy responses.

BODY -- - BRAIN

Interpret with senses, previous experiences, triggers from the nerves, Diet, Exercise, Substance Abuse, Slecp Quality, Cognitive Decline, and Injuries challenge every person to question their decision-making. The persons who embrace the Objective Truth of Holy Scripture refuse to let the Brain be the only deciding factor.

BODY --- 5 SENSES

SIGHT, SMELL, HEARING, TASTE, TOUCH can influence, as described earlier in the book. When a person chooses to align the Soul with the Spirit to overshadow the five senses or determine how the senses can echo the beliefs and thoughts, then that person aligns his five senses with the Objective Truth, Holy Scripture, to live a more stable and sane life.

BODY --- NERVES, DNA

Impulses of muscles or organs, bundles of fibers that send and receive messages between the body and the brain, nervous agitation or irritability, heart rate dysfunction, blood pressure, irregular temperature, bladder problems, and headaches.

While Butyrate may help in some way, a person who chooses to accept the OBJECTIVE TRUTH of the Gospel and renews their mind then that person is empowered to walk in the newness of life with extraordinary strength from GOD to keep their body proper.

BODY --- LOVE --- SEXUALITY

Infidelity, watching Pornography, im-pure thoughts, and drama, morally wrong activities. Objective Truth: Romans 12 says not to conform to the pattern of this world but to be transformed by the renewing of your mind. This can happen when a wise person finds the prescribed meds that can manage or lower the sex drive and control the serotonin and dopamine levels.

BODY --- STREET DRUGS CONSUMED

Heroin, Cocaine, Methamphetamines, LSD, Hallucinogens, Marijuana (weed), Ecstasy, Ketamine, Crack. These drugs affect all different types of people in a lot of different ways. When these people choose to live by strong beliefs and not strong drugs, then they experience a more constructive outcome. For each of us, it has to be brought to our attention.

BODY --- ALCOHOL DRINKING CONSUMED

VODKA, BEER, WHISKEY, CLASSIC COCKTAILS, RUM, TEQUILA, and more. Those who consume these drinks are only thinking about themselves. Unfortunately, the bigger picture must be brought to their attention, which is done by the working of the 3 concentric circles.

THESE COMPONENTS OF THE BODY, ALONG WITH THE EXTERNAL TRIGGERS, CAN CAUSE REACTIVE BEHAVIORS, BUT THE PERSON WHO EMBRACES THE OBJECTIVE TRUTH AND FOLLOWS THE CORRECT WORKING OF THE 3 CONCENTRIC CIRCLES EXPERIENCES TRANSFORMATION.

By the same token, some evidence suggests that praising character as opposed to behavior is a more effective means of promoting positive behaviors. For example, in one study, children who were told that they were helpful people for doing something generous (donating some of their marbles to poor children) later engaged in more altruistic behavior than children whose behavior alone was praised or who did not receive praise.

NOW, IN CONCLUSION, THE 3 PARTS OF A HUMAN

"Now may the God of peace make you holy in every way, and may your whole spirit and soul and body be kept blameless until our Lord Jesus Christ comes again."

1 Thessalonians 5:23

SECTION ·8·

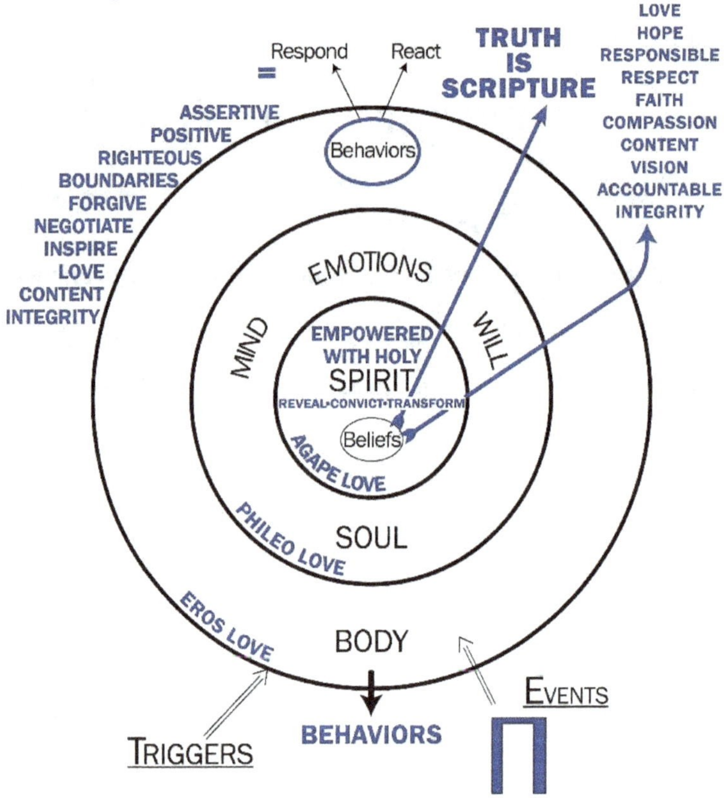

Respond
React
=
TRUTH IS SCRIPTURE
LOVE
HOPE
RESPONSIBLE
RESPECT
FAITH
COMPASSION
CONTENT
VISION
ACCOUNTABLE
INTEGRITY
ASSERTIVE
POSITIVE
RIGHTEOUS
BOUNDARIES
FORGIVE
NEGOTIATE
INSPIRE
LOVE
CONTENT
INTEGRITY
Behaviors
EMOTIONS
MIND
WILL
EMPOWERED WITH HOLY
SPIRIT
REVEAL·CONVICT·TRANSFORM
Beliefs
AGAPE LOVE
PHILEO LOVE
SOUL
EROS LOVE
BODY
BEHAVIORS
TRIGGERS
EVENTS

SECTION # 8 - *BEHAVIORS* –

When a person agrees with the objective TRUTH, the TRUTH from the Creator, that person has become empowered/equipped with the Spirit to impart wisdom to the Soul's WILL, which in turn directs the Body to RESPOND, not React to life's events. (See the Diagram)

The Essence of the WILL in the Soul:

1. Cravings 2. Urges 3. Decisions 4. Moral conviction 5. Morally enslaved 6. Desires 7. Affections 8. Vows 9. Loyalty 10. Selfishness 11. Dedicate 12. Trust 13. Respect 14. Forgive 15. Determine 16. Promote 17. Reconcile 18. Perspective 19. Lead 20. Follow 21. Obedience 22. Declare 23. Restore 24. Trajectory

These characteristics, empowered by Objective Truth, acknowledged by the Heart, and manifested by the Mind, motivate these characteristics to behave responsibly.

When a person decides to humble and surrender self to acknowledge their need for a Higher Power and desire to become a member of the family of God by means of confession of sin, celebrating the heart change with baptism, and growing to become a disciple, then that person will respond not react to life's encounters.

RESPOND: 3 components

ASSERTIVE - Humility, Offer Ideas and Disagree Respectfully, Appreciation, Influence, Calmness, Direct

POSITIVE – Self-Confidence without Arrogance, Peaceful, Loyal, Mindful, Content, Confident, Respect

DECISIVE - Boundaries, Compromise, Negotiate, Problem-Solver, Reasoning, Learn from Experiences, Trust

1 Thessalonians 5:23 says, "May your whole spirit, soul, and body be kept blameless at the coming of our Lord Jesus Christ."

No person has their own strength, power, or perseverance to live out these Response components. Because a person chooses to live the values and principles of God's Holy Bible, that person is granted the mercy and grace to become empowered with extraordinary strength to live out these Respond components.

Parents, are your children and teens demonstrating these characteristics in their daily lives? If not, that's why they need you to show them the way to a content life. These are the qualities every person who is a member of God's family should display and live as a testimony of God's will and purpose for all believers.

RESPOND – defined: as saying something in reply to an action or statement. Response is more thoughtful and done with reasoning. People who respond put their thoughts ahead of their actions. Remember the old saying: "Put your mind in gear before you put your mouth in motion." People think and formulate an intelligent and suitable reply before going vocal or physical. Consider your options! Do you want to be identified as one who is impulsive or one who is thoughtful and intelligent?

RESPOND == ASSERTIVE = Humility, Boundaries, Compromise, Negotiate, Reasoning, Appreciation, Influence, Calmness, Confident, Respect, Trust, or Direct

One example: A situation where someone who gets laid off from work naturally gets initially upset, which is a normal **reaction**. How long somebody remains upset and how intense the feelings present are influenced by a person's belief based upon the TRUTH the person has embraced. Those with healthier secondary **responses** are able to adjust more quickly. The healthier cognitive **response** is to remind yourself that you have skills and abilities that employers want, to tell yourself not to lose hope, and to tell yourself that you will be able to find another job; just try your best.

The unhealthier **reaction** is to continue being emotionally upset.

The healthier cognitive **response** leads to more positivity, less emotional stress, increased effectiveness, and more energy to problem-solve.

To help the reader understand more clearly, a s**econd example** is where two different people find out that they have been diagnosed with high blood pressure. Similarly, both people **react** by getting upset, but one person lets this **reaction** continue in a negative way, whereas the other person **responds** and copes with the problem more effectively in the long run. The healthier cognitive **response** includes positive self-talk and optimism, which ultimately increases the likelihood of healthy behaviors such as eating healthier food and exercising regularly. The healthier and more **responsive** self-dialog includes saying to oneself, "It will be okay. I'm going to eat better and exercise more to manage my high blood pressure!"

EXAMPLES OF RESPONSIVENESS OF BEHAVIORS IN THE BODY:

BODY --- CHEMICAL IMBALANCES

Anxiety, ADD, ADHD, ASTHMA, Diabetes, High blood pressure, Hypertension, NEUROTRANSMITTERS like Serotonins & Dopamine high Testosterone level, Estrogen level, Lymph nodes, Peptic Ulcer, Schizophrenia, Hormone imbalance.

When faced with Life's Triggers and Events, if the person has addressed the medical necessity of the mentioned chemical imbalances and has embraced the Objective Truth of Holy Scripture, then the person acknowledges: 1. PURPOSE (Aim) 2. MEANINGFULNESS (Significance) and 3. SELF-IMAGE (Dignity).

BODY -- - BRAIN

The person who embraces the Objective Truth of Holy Scripture in their heart and demonstrates positive thinking communicates to his Will that he is physically empowered and also mentally empowered to exhibit assertive, positive, and decisive responses toward sanity and constructive outcomes rather than just letting the brain be the deciding factor.

BODY --- 5 SENSES

SIGHT, SMELL, HEARING, TASTE, TOUCH can influence, as described earlier in the book. When a person chooses to align the Soul with the Spirit by incorporating Objective Truth and holy Scripture, the Mind directs the five senses to live a more stable, secure, and sensible life.

BODY --- NERVES, DNA

A person who chooses to accept the OBJECTIVE TRUTH of the Gospel in their heart and renew their mind then that person is empowered to not let his nerves or organs dictate his reactions but Godly principles to walk in the newness of life with extraordinary strength from GOD.

BODY --- LOVE

Objective Truth: Romans 12 says not to conform to the pattern of this world but to be transformed by the renewing of your mind. When the transformation occurs, the person gains knowledge that there are three types of Love: Unconditional Love, Conditional Love, and Erotic Love. Now, it will be imperative for the person to be trained with specifics and examples of these three types of Responses to communicate well, with respect, and with trust in built-in relationships.

BODY --- STREET DRUGS CONSUMED & ALCOHOL DRINKING CONSUMED

As a person evaluates the effects of their consumption of drugs or drinking, the working of the 3 concentric circles will bring to their attention to create transformation from the inside outward. So, the person will acknowledge the Objective Truth to establish a solid belief system in their heart. The next step is to allow the heart to reconstruct the Soul. The person chooses to direct the nervous system and endocrine system to exhibit assertive, positive, and decisive responses to cope with life without the need for substances.

Recall the seven scenarios presented in Section 3 of this book. With the help of this counselor, you, the reader, will see how the introduction to Objective Truth in Section 5 created a much different spirit and soul and different Behaviors in this Section for the persons in these seven stories.

SCENARIO # 1: Regarding one of my clients, he shared that he leaves work and stops by the bar to get a drink of Vodka to calm him from his busy day at work and to face his demanding wife. The combination of the thoughts in his mind and the emotions in his amygdala causes his desire (will) to consume the Vodka after work.

With the help of this counselor, Belief # ***9. Urge Self-control* --- 2 Peter 1**

With the installment of this new objective truth, the Client learned to add to his faith, goodness; and to goodness, knowledge, and to knowledge, self-control, and to self-control, perseverance; and to perseverance, godliness; verse 8 - for if you possess these qualities, they will keep you from being ineffective and unproductive.

SCENARIO #2 SQUEAKY WHEEL GETS THE GREASE ---

With the help of this counselor, Belief # ***6. Plant TRUTH which can save from filth ---*** *James 1:21* inserted.

So, this Client established his protocol to understand God's wisdom. Understanding God is not the same as being book-smart or street-smart. By applying Scripture concepts (James 1:21), the squeaky wheel person now rids their life of moral filth and accepts a more humble state, which demonstrates respect, not selfishness.

SCENARIO # 3 WORLDLY TRUTH IMPACTS FALSE BELIEFS ---- The Client has said that he had no part in the demise of his three previous marriages.

With the guidance of this counselor, Belief # ***3. Transforms the Mind*** **--** *Romans 12:2* was engaged.

This client learned not to accept false beliefs and not conform to the patterns of this world, but his mind transformed from stinking thinking to accepting responsibility that his past is impacting his current marriage.

SCENARIO # 4 EMPHASIS ON BELIEFS:

This Therapist showed the Client how his belief of getting away with the encounters with the female co-worker shaped his thoughts and feelings on this last encounter and caused his will to set his behaviors to go further with a sexual intimate encounter with this girl. So, this is why the Client committed the Infidelity and now is troubled by the guilt, shame, and pain of hurting his wife.

With the help of this Counselor, Belief # ***15. Show Respect*** – Romans 12:9—Love must be sincere. Hate what is evil; cling to what is good. Be devoted to one another in love. Honor one another above yourselves.

SCENARIO # 5 ***Narcissistic Personality Disorder*** (NPD) Their BELIEF SYSTEM manifests grandiose fantasies about themselves (i.e., *they're smarter, more attractive, and more successful than everyone they know*)

With the help of this counselor, Belief # ***4. Sheds light on one's inmost being --*** According to 2 Timothy, the narcissist comes to realize that his characteristics are not working for him and must humble himself to believe differently so he responds to life, not react.

SCENARIO # 6 The Client conveys to this Therapist that she feels she's no longer pretty because of her gray hair and the change in her body contour.

The client did not realize that her thoughts were actually her beliefs. She said no one has ever shown her that in the past. With the help of this Counselor, Belief # ***10. Presents Integrity ---*** 1 Peter 3:3 Your Beauty should not come from outward adornment. Rather, it should be that of your inner self, the unfading beauty of a gentle and quiet spirit. This new belief about herself resulted in greater confidence in her cognition, evoked much healthier feelings about herself, and did not react to her husband's perspective.

SCENARIO #7: EXAMPLE: Counseling sessions with Dave (the name is changed to comply with HIPPA) With the help of this Counselor, Belief #***20 – Responsibility – Galatians 6 & #21 – Kindness - Galatians 5:22***

So, this Therapist encouraged the Client to Respond in an assertive way to care for all the children if his wife passes from this life.

Results – this is what is supposed to happen with the objective truth of the Holy Scriptures incorporated to bring about constructive change in behaviors

Compliance with Holy Scripture brings about constructive change in the following ways:

1. Demonstrate healthy coping skills to use to cope with depression, anxiety, or stress by responding and not reacting to triggers.

2. Assess and determine the causes for the inability to perform well in work and relationships. Present incorporation of truth to gain strength and wisdom to make and adjust disposition to demonstrate significant changes

3. Incorporate the TRUTH of Galatians 5: 22 to help disposition toward clarity, reasonable actions, measurable goals, and behaviors that effect positive change

4. Impulse control: The conscious presentation to manage urges or delay gratification. Articulate the Triggers that lead to poor impulse control.

5. Show measurable differences in behaviors in the quality of life by maintaining ongoing abstinence from all mood-altering chemicals, self – actualization, healthy communication, correcting narcissism, abstinence from recreational drinks or drugs, mental stability, or stopping binge eating to cope.

6. Ct will demonstrate strong, healthy belief systems and wise decision-making toward healthy and effective outcomes

7. Challenge NEGATIVE THOUGHTS and REPLACE with POSITIVE thoughts and feelings.

With a positive and powerful Christian belief system, a Believer can achieve (Colossians 1:10-14 CEVDCI) in this world. This positive belief system comes from the presentation and incorporation of the Objective Truth of the Holy Scriptures.

TALENTS AND GIFTS -- BEHAVIORS

Talents and spiritual gifts are from God. Both grow in effectiveness with use. Both are intended to be used in service to others, not for selfish purposes. First Corinthians 12:7 states that spiritual gifts are given to benefit others and not ourselves.

Spiritual gifts are given to all believers by the Holy Spirit (Romans 12:3, 6) at the time they place their faith in Christ for the forgiveness of their sins. A person (belief in God or in Christ) is given a natural talent as a result of a combination of genetics (some have a natural ability in music, art, or mathematics) and surroundings (growing up in a musical family will aid one in developing a talent for music), or because God desired to endow certain individuals with certain talents (for example, Bezalel in Exodus 31:1-6).

Romans 12:3-8 lists the spiritual gifts as follows: prophecy, serving others (in a general sense), teaching, exhorting, generosity, leadership, and showing mercy.

First Corinthians 12:8-11 lists the gifts as the word of wisdom (ability to communicate spiritual wisdom), the word of knowledge (ability to communicate practical truth), faith (unusual reliance upon God)… furtherance of the Gospel of Christ.

All are called and equipped to be involved in the "work of the ministry" (Ephesians 4:12). All are gifted so that they can contribute to the cause of Christ out of gratitude for all He has done for them. In doing so, they also find fulfillment in life through their service to Christ.

(BEHAVIORS) Respond, not React. The Spirit conflicts with fleshly desires, so you shouldn't do whatever you want to do. (Galatians 5:16-17 CEB). Let your light shine before others so that they may see your good deeds and glorify your Father in heaven. (Matthew 5:16)

God has given us his precious promises… for this very reason, make every effort to add to your faith, goodness; and to goodness, knowledge; and to knowledge, self-control; and to self-control, perseverance; and to perseverance, godliness; and to godliness, mutual affection; and to mutual affection, unconditional love. For if you possess these qualities, they will keep you from being ineffective and unproductive…(2 Peter 1: 4 -8).

For a person to experience a new life, this person must not try to transform their life from the outside inward but to transform life from the inside outward.

When a person is faced with life's triggers and events, that person must not listen to the brain in the body or the five senses that cause the behavior to react. Instead, when a person is faced with these life's triggers and situations, the person must look deep inside his heart as to what he believes. Those beliefs come from a certain truth. However,

along the way, spiritual and secular dynamics can sway the person's mind to listen to his brain and let his emotions dictate his reactions. The person must explore the beliefs in his heart, which affect the thinking in his mind and the emotions in his amygdala, which then impacts the will in the soul to create a different set of behaviors in the body, which is responding to life, not reacting to life's triggers and events.

SUMMARY – MY BOOK

With the three concentric circles diagram in your hand, it will help you understand the summary completely. See the diagrams below.

The goal of this author is to inform the reader that a person is possessed by 3 Characteristics: body, soul, and spirit. (See bottom of diagram) When a person is confronted with the triggers (verbal abuse, etc.) and events of life, they impact these three characteristics of a human being. How a person handles these three characteristics of themselves causes the person to exhibit one of the two types of behaviors: react (negative) or respond (positive). If the person's body is not in the right condition because of chemical imbalance (ADHD),

unhealthy nerves, the impact of the five senses (sight, smell, hearing, taste, and touch) which cause interpretation of the brain, or deficiencies of sleep/ eat or exercise, and the impact of street drugs and alcoholic drinking, then these elements of the body influence the soul elements (mind, emotions, and will) and the beliefs in the heart which result in the person to react (negatively) or respond (positively) in their behaviors.

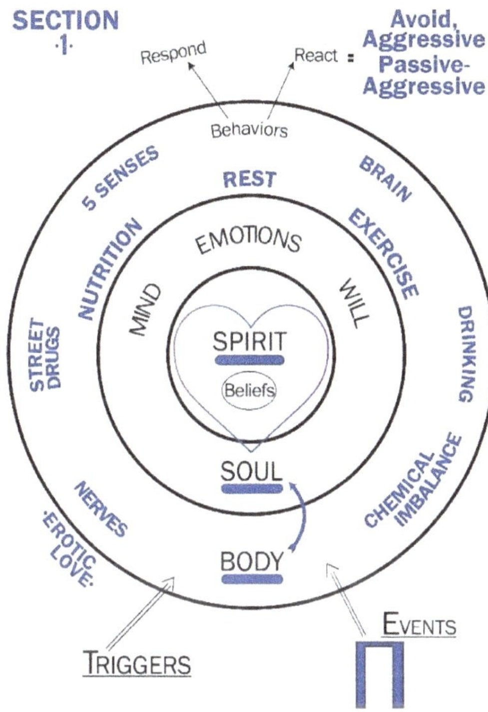

Most people believe if they change from the <u>outside inward,</u> such as changing the elements and the characteristics of the body (see above), then it will impact what they think and how they feel, which inspires the person to react to life's events and life's triggers that the person is faced with.

The purpose and goal of this author/ counselor is to inform the person that they are not to react but to respond to life's events and triggers. So, to make this change, the person must initiate change from the <u>inside outward.</u>

SECTION ·3·

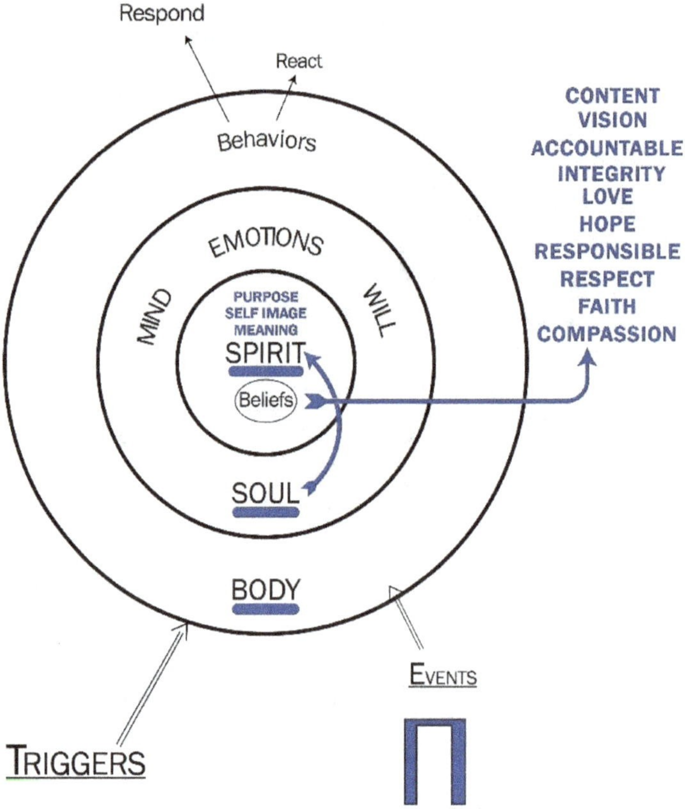

When the person is faced with these life's triggers (see diagram), the person must first examine the beliefs (i.e., integrity, etc.) in his heart. Is the person empowered with healthy beliefs or false beliefs in the spirit of their heart? Can you see that healthy or false beliefs strongly influence the soul elements, which inevitably cause one of the two types of behaviors?

This author/counselor inquires of the person if they exhibit the BELIEF qualities: Love, Hope, Honor, Responsibility, Respect, Faith, Compassion, Content, Vision, Accountability, and Integrity. The beliefs developed inside of a person's heart come from two different types of truth: Subjective truth and Objective truth. The person presenting unhealthy belief qualities acquires them from the Subjective Truth. Likewise, the person presenting healthy belief qualities acquires them from Objective Truth.

Subjective truth is based on a person's perspective, senses, opinions, and experiences. Objective truth is based on the reality that exists independently of beliefs, opinions, or perceptions. It is true regardless of whether anyone believes it or not.

For this person to make the necessary or desired changes begins with incorporating the objective truth to present the healthy Belief qualities mentioned. These belief qualities in the heart influence the mind in the soul and the brain in the body, emotions manifested, and direct the Will (see diagram) to communicate to the body to respond to life's triggers.

RESPOND: 3 components

ASSERTIVE - Humility, Offer Ideas and Disagree Respectfully, Appreciation, Influence, Calmness, Direct

POSITIVE – Self-Confidence without Arrogance, Peaceful, Loyal, Mindful, Content, Confident, Respect

DECISIVE - Boundaries, Compromise, Negotiate, Problem-Solver, Reasoning, Learn from Experiences, Trust

To the reader, Question: would other people state that you display these qualities? If not, these qualities come from incorporating the Objective Truth of the Holy Scriptures, which is true regardless of whether anyone believes it or not. Start today to embrace the truth of the Gospel to experience radical transformation to a stable, vibrant life.

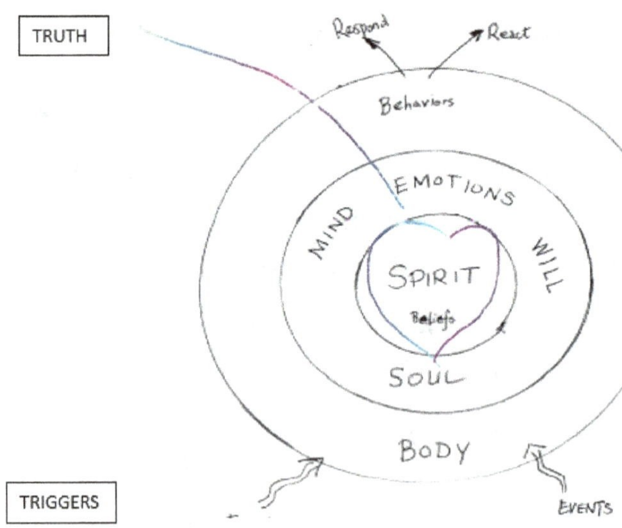

There are two different types of behaviors: React or Respond

1. React, which is passive, aggressive, passive-aggressive.

2. Respond, which is to be assertive and decisive. Assertive is to negotiate, express self-confidence, compromise, and set proper boundaries. Most contemporary persons operate out of their secular mind by reacting to life's triggers and are not aware of the bigger picture, the 3 concentric circles.

Everyone is faced with life's triggers and life's events that impact the body. From the 3 Concentric Circles diagram, the BODY is the first portion to explore. If the body is not in the right condition, it will react to the triggers and events. So, if a person has a chemical imbalance, then he needs to consume prescribed meds to be conditioned properly. If the person has not consumed the right amount of food sleep, or engaged in proper exercise, then he must improve his routine to cope with life's triggers. With a fleshly desire to consume street drugs or strong drinks, then the person's physical disposition will influence the Soul.

The SOUL is the second part of a person. The soul is made up of three parts: mind, emotions, and will. The mind and the brain are different. The Brain is in the body, and the mind is in the soul. If the mind is listening to the body, then it creates stinking thinking from the five senses or DNA. This thinking causes unhealthy emotions or feelings. The second part of the Soul is the emotions from the Amygdala. Most individuals who operate the Secular Mind allow their emotions to behave in a reactive sort of way.

The Will, the third part of the soul, is made up of the nerve system and the endocrine system, which interprets the mind and the emotions to impact and influence the behaviors of the body.

The SPIRIT is the third part of a person. The spirit is not located in the actual physical heart or chest. However, the spirit is positioned in what is described as the heart, where a person's belief system exists. One must consider what is the Truth embraced that creates a certain type of belief system that impacts decisions. Every person must consider and incorporate the healthy objective truth found outside the body, soul, and spirit, which sets up a person's right belief system.

TRUTH is the basis and foundation of how people should act, how people should make decisions, and have healthy relationships with others.

When the Soul agrees with the Spirit by aligning with the TRUTH, double-mindedness does not occur. TRUTH will manifest itself in the physical body, displayed as peace, constructive power, patience, and perseverance, which lead to victory, joy, prosperity, endurance, and the ability to respond to life in healthy ways.

To make the necessary transformation for a much healthier life, it is necessary to make changes from the inside out (see the diagram), not to make the changes from the outside inward.

First, to start from the inside, this therapist encourages every person to consider, evaluate, and reevaluate beliefs based on the objective truth each person embraces. Most people do not embrace the correct type of truth.

Second, for each reader to begin the transformation, the reader must use the worksheet within the Book to discover, identify, and acknowledge their core beliefs, then determine where or how the reader arrived at their core beliefs from what Truth embraced.

Third, for every reader to embrace a solid, stable, and sane belief system, the reader will find greater benefit and effective outcomes when the reader invests in the core values and principles of the TRUTH, Holy Scripture/ Holy Bible. Everyone should realize there is a superior creator for this world to function reasonably. When the reader agrees with objective TRUTH, the TRUTH from the Creator, that person has become empowered/equipped with the Holy Spirit to impart wisdom to the Soul, which in turn directs the Body to RESPOND, not React to life's events, which should be the goal of every person.

Fourth, (SPIRIT) God has given the reader the Holy Spirit by faith, which imparts unconditional love (Romans 5:5) in the spirit of His children. His Truth lets all persons know that because of Christ's suffering, believers will be given what God has promised (Romans 8:16-18). The person who incorporates the Scriptural Truth is empowered to overcome a secular mindset and embrace extraordinary strength from God's Spirit that lives in a person's spirit (Romans 8:9-10).

Fifth, (MIND) a believer with God's spirit empowers the transformation of the Mind from stinking thinking to reasonable thinking, conforms values from perceived

truth to objective truth, pursues contentment versus happiness, empowered to freely choose to honor the Creator, develops perseverance to become mature and not lack wisdom, free of doubts, eradicate toxic thoughts. Faith in the Son of God is what gives each believer this victory to overcome the insanity of the world. (1 John 5:4).

Sixth, (EMOTIONS) So deaden the power of the evil desires lurking in your body, such as Sexual immorality, moral corruption, lust, evil desire, and greed. But now, set aside anger, rage, malice, slander, obscene language, lies. Put on the new nature which is renewed in knowledge. Choose the emotions of compassion, kindness, humility, gentleness, patience, tolerance, peace, thankfulness, and forgiveness. And over these virtues put on love, which binds them all together in perfect unity. (Colossians 3:5-14 CEB)

Seventh, (WILL) God's word is alive and powerful. It is sharper than any double-edged sword. His word can cut through our spirit and soul, through our joints and marrow, until it discovers the desires and thoughts of our soul. (Hebrews 4:12) As a result, they don't live the rest of their human lives determined by human desires but in ways determined by God's Will. (Peter 4:2 CEB). When a person chose freely to be compelled to sin, what consequences did that person receive for doing things that now ashamed of?

(Romans 6) His friends might say to him: How is that working for you? But now, being made free from sin and becoming servants to God by your own free Will, you have your fruit in holiness. (Romans 6: 22 KJV)

Eighth, (BEHAVIORS) Respond, not React. The Spirit conflicts with fleshly desires, so you shouldn't do whatever you want to do. (Galatians 5:16-17 CEB). Let your light shine before others so that they may see your good deeds and glorify your Father in heaven. (Matthew 5:16)

God has given us his precious promises... for this very reason, make every effort to add to your faith, goodness; and to goodness, knowledge; and to knowledge, self-control; and to self-control, perseverance; and to perseverance, godliness; and to godliness, mutual affection; and to mutual affection, unconditional love. For if you possess these qualities, they will keep you from being ineffective and unproductive...(2 Peter 1: 4 -8).

GREATER SUMMARY OF THE GOAL: By embracing the TRUTH of Holy Scripture, the presence of the Holy Spirit in a person's spirit empowers the reader with extraordinary strength and a new set of beliefs that change the thoughts of the mind and controls the emotions of the Soul. So, the endocrine and nerve systems of the Will

direct the body's behaviors to respond, not react, in addressing life's triggers and events for the benefit of making a radical transformation to a healthier, more vibrant life.

M. KEITH HENSON

AUTHOR/ LMFT COUNSELOR

PHONE: 832-207-6064

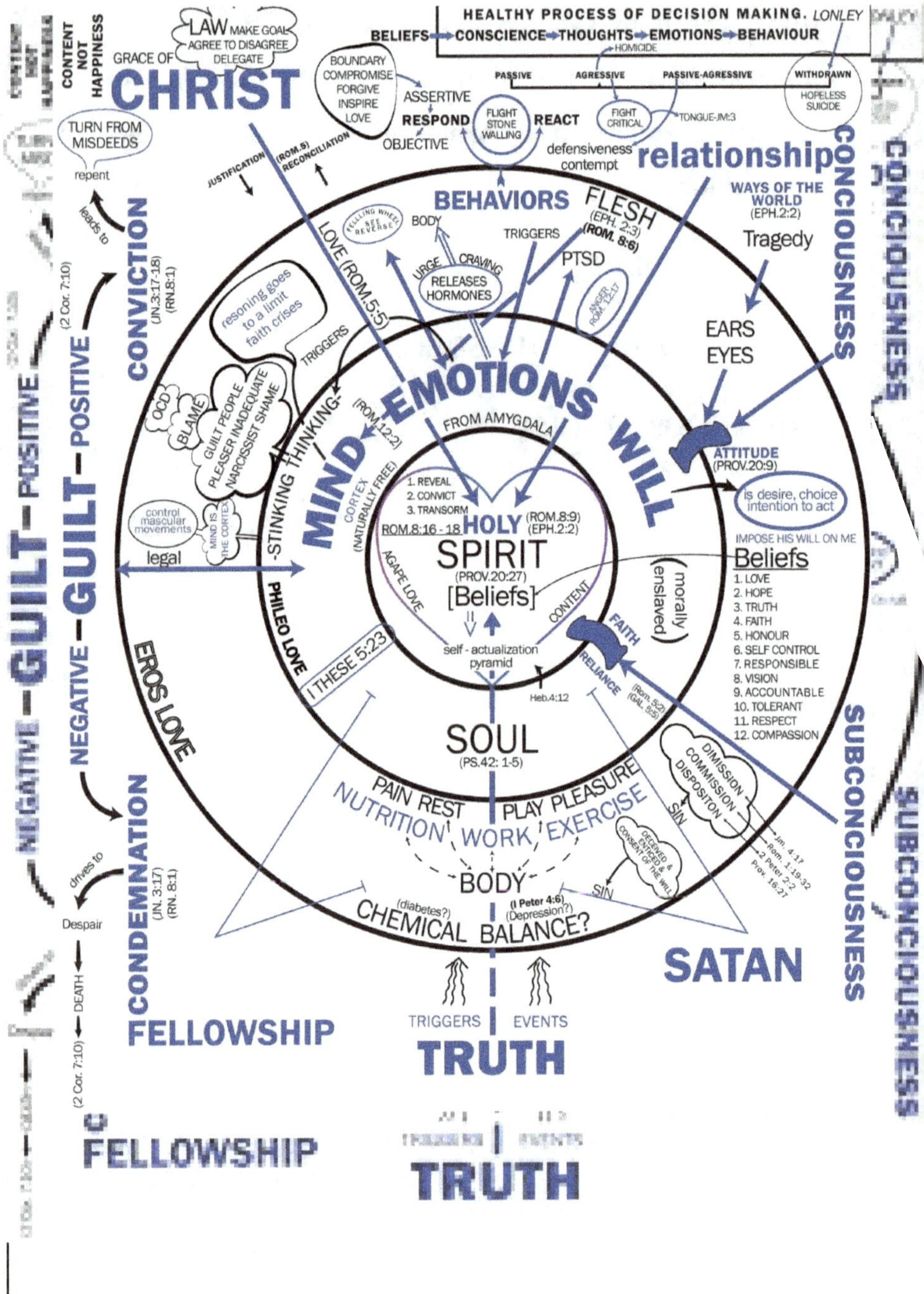

HEALTHY PROCESS OF DECISION MAKING. LONLEY
BELIEFS → CONSCIENCE → THOUGHTS → EMOTIONS → BEHAVIOUR
HOMICIDE
PASSIVE
AGRESSIVE
PASSIVE-AGRESSIVE
WITHDRAWN
HOPELESS SUICIDE
LAW MAKE GOAL AGREE TO DISAGREE DELEGATE
GRACE OF
CHRIST
CONTENT NOT HAPPINESS
BOUNDARY COMPROMISE FORGIVE INSPIRE LOVE
ASSERTIVE
RESPOND
OBJECTIVE
FLIGHT STONE WALLING
REACT
FIGHT CRITICAL
TONGUE-JM:3
defensiveness contempt
relationship
TURN FROM MISDEEDS
repent
leads to
JUSTIFICATION (ROM.5) RECONCILIATION
CONVICTION (JN.3:17-18) (RN.8:1)
(2 Cor. 7:10)
BEHAVIORS
FLESH (EPH. 2:3) (ROM. 8:6)
WAYS OF THE WORLD (EPH.2:2)
Tragedy
BODY
TRIGGERS
PTSD
URGE CRAVING
RELEASES HORMONES
LOVE (ROM.5:5)
resoning goes to a limit faith crises
TRIGGERS
ANGER ROM. 12:17
EARS EYES
CONCIOUSNESS
EMOTIONS
OCD
BLAME
GUILT PEOPLE PLEASER INADEQUATE NARCISSIST SHAME
(ROM.12:2)
FROM AMYGDALA
WILL
ATTITUDE (PROV.20:9)
is desire, choice intention to act
NEGATIVE - GUILT - POSITIVE
STINKING THINKING
MIND
CORTEX (NATURALLY FREE)
1. REVEAL
2. CONVICT
3. TRANSORM
ROM.8:16 - 18
HOLY (ROM.8:9) (EPH.2:2)
SPIRIT (PROV.20:27)
[Beliefs]
control mascular movements
MIND IS THE CORTEX
legal
AGAPE LOVE
CONTENT
IMPOSE HIS WILL ON ME
Beliefs
1. LOVE
2. HOPE
3. TRUTH
4. FAITH
5. HONOUR
6. SELF CONTROL
7. RESPONSIBLE
8. VISION
9. ACCOUNTABLE
10. TOLERANT
11. RESPECT
12. COMPASSION
(morally enslaved)
PHILEO LOVE
EROS LOVE
I THESE 5:23
self - actualization pyramid
Heb.4:12
FAITH
RELIANCE
(Rom. 5:2) (GAL. 5:5)
SOUL (PS.42: 1-5)
DIMISSION COMMISSION DISPOSITON
SIN
SUBCONCIOUSNESS
PAIN REST
PLAY PLEASURE
NUTRITION WORK EXERCISE
BODY
DECEIVED & ENTICED & CONSENT OF THE WILL
SIN
Jm. 4:17
Rom. 1:19-32
2 Peter 2:2
Prov. 16:27
(diabetes?)
(I Peter 4:6) (Depression?)
CHEMICAL BALANCE?
CONDEMNATION (JN. 3:17) (RN. 8:1)
drives to
Despair
DEATH
(2 Cor. 7:10)
SATAN
TRIGGERS
EVENTS
FELLOWSHIP
TRUTH

www.ingramcontent.com/pod-product-compliance
Lightning Source LLC
LaVergne TN
LVHW022218200926
848481LV00006B/2024
* 9 7 9 8 8 6 9 3 4 4 9 5 3 *